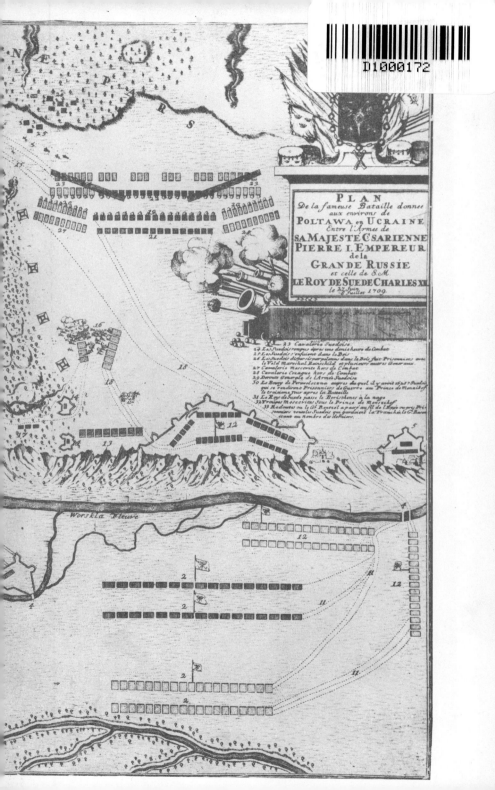

HETMAN
OF
UKRAINE
IVAN MAZEPPA

HETMAN
OF
UKRAINE
Ivan Mazeppa

By CLARENCE A. MANNING

NEW YORK : BOOKMAN ASSOCIATES, PUBLISHERS

MANUFACTURED IN THE UNITED STATES OF AMERICA
PRINTED BY RECORD PRESS, NEW YORK, N. Y.

DEDICATED TO THE MEMORY OF

Dr. Luke Myshuha

EDITOR OF SVOBODA

A CHAMPION OF UKRAINIAN INDEPENDENCE

AND

A PATRIOTIC AMERICAN

TABLE OF CONTENTS

CHAPTER ONE

REVOLUTION IN MOSCOW

In the first days of August, 1689, a brilliant cavalcade was approaching Moscow over one of the main roads that led to the capital from Ukraine. At its head rode in all the state and dignity of his position, Ivan Mazeppa, the Hetman of the Zaporozhian Host and of Ukraine, and behind came the general officers of the Host and five of the regimental colonels, each with his own lesser officers and their staffs. All in all the number of persons of rank and prominence numbered more than three hundred men and these were followed by a detachment of Kozak troops and personal servants. It seemed more like a small army than a delegation on a peaceful mission.

It was a splendid group of men. The Hetman, mounted on a spirited horse, carried the mace, the symbol of his office, and ahead of him a high ranking officer carried the bunchuk, the horsetail standard of the Hetman. Mazeppa, a man apparently in his fifties, carried himself with a poise and dignity which even overshadowed the splendor of the scarlet tunics, the superb horses and their costly trappings. Every detail was meticulously perfect and the same care had been expended on the uniforms of all down to the lowest private, the ordinary Kozaks and to the long train of carts that lumbered along in the rear and which seemed to be carrying valuable loads, if one could judge from the strict guard that was kept over them.

Every movement of the Hetman indicated that he was well conscious of his own rank and intended to have that rank recognized by all with whom he came into personal contact, even if they happened to be his superiors, and who could be above him but the Tsar himself? Never had a foreign sovereign or a vassal prince approached Moscow with such formality and pomp, and as the procession passed the various squalid villages, the peasants paused to wonder at this array of fine costumes, which far surpassed in beauty even the outfits of the Tsars.

The Hetman rode along, buried in his own thoughts and he seemed utterly oblivious of his own companions and the passers-by, who again and again muttered maledictions on this obviously non-Muscovite cavalcade which was daring to approach holy Moscow.

The march was apparently well timed, for as the travellers came in sight of the capital and the grim walls of the Kremlin, they found awaiting them a group of high Muscovite officials, likewise with their subordinates and troops to extend an equally formal welcome. Here too was the Tsar's own coach, which had been sent by the special orders of the Regent, the Tsarevna Sofia, to meet the Hetman and to conduct him in proper state to the quarters that had been prepared for him and his higher officers within the carefully guarded walls of the Kremlin.

The proper formalities were carried out, formal greetings were exchanged, and then the Hetman dismounted and entered the coach. The escorts reformed and the march was resumed. Progress now was much slower for the column was moving through the narrow and winding streets of the city, but finally it reached its destination in the very centre of the tsarist power.

Here Prince Vasili Golitsyn was waiting to greet his old friend and comrade in arms and to deliver to Mazeppa a personal welcome from the Tsarevna. She was the ruling power in Moscow. Prince Golitsyn was her lover as well as her most important general and statesman. The marks of honor which the two bestowed upon the visiting Hetman spoke volumes of the esteem in which he was held at the Muscovite court and of the respect of that court for his ability and power.

The next days were filled with a succession of feasts and banquets and formal receptions. Prince Golitsyn, the most cultured man in Moscow, had long been under the influence of the scholars of Kiev. He knew both Latin and Polish and he and Mazeppa vied with each other in delivering long and flowery eulogies of each other's services in the campaign against the Crimea. Entertainment succeeded to entertainment. The Tsarevna Sofia, herself well educated for a Muscovite lady of the day, joined in and all seemed happy and gay.

Yet Mazeppa did not forget the proprieties of the occasion. He carefully presented his respects to the two Tsars, the almost imbecile Ivan and his half-brother Peter and he did not seem to notice that while Ivan listened unintelligently to his florid oration, Peter had refused to meet him and stayed sullenly away. This was in fact a deliberate insult but Mazeppa knew that two years earlier when Golitsyn had returned from his expedition against Perekop in the Crimea, Peter had likewise obstinately refused to see him. Mazeppa was in Moscow on an official visit to the Tsars, the Regent and Prince Golitsyn to whom he was beholden for his post as Hetman and he deliberately shut his eyes and ears to all that was going on around him.

That was plenty. The court and indeed the whole of Moscow was seething with discontent and intrigue which was barely concealed. Again and again as Mazeppa and his party had travelled through the Muscovite villages, he could not fail to overhear the muttered curses of the pious Great Russians on the Little Russian[1] dogs who had perverted the teachings of the Orthodox Church through their influence on the Patriarch Nikon and who had brought about the imprisonment and martyrdom of the holy Avvakum who in the name of the Old Faith had struggled against the innovations of the Greeks and the Kievans. And here was a Hetman from Kiev coming to holy Moscow to cast still more enchantments upon pious and all-Christian Moscow, the centre of the world and of Orthodoxy.

The peasants were not alone in this. The streltsy, the permanent Muscovite army, who had come out by order of the Regent to greet Mazeppa, were even more bitter. They had been cowed by Sofia into silence but wherever they felt themselves unwatched and free to speak, they added their maledictions to those that were being

---

[1] At this period the Muscovites contemptuously called the Ukrainians Little Russians.

poured out on the Ukrainian Hetman by all classes of the population. Mazeppa calmly ignored all the insults.

Yet this deep-rooted Muscovite opposition to all things foreign and Western was as nothing in comparison with the feud within the Kremlin itself between the Miloslavsky family and the Naryshkins. Sofia and the imbecile Ivan were the children of Tsar Alexis by his first wife, a Miloslavsky. Peter and his mother, the second wife of Alexis, were Naryshkins. The Miloslavsky faction was in control but Peter was coming of age. He was nearly eight feet tall and while he apparently took no interest in affairs of state, it was feared that he and his mother's family would soon be in a position to exert tremendous influence. The partisans of the two families were coming to blows in the streets and no one knew when the coming explosion would break through the iron curtain of Muscovite formalism.

Under such conditions the visit of the Hetman of Ukraine could not fail to arouse comment, especially when it became known that Peter had refused to meet him and that Mazeppa on all possible occasions was making long speeches in honor of Prince Golitsyn who was of course deeply involved with the Miloslavsky faction.

The gossip spread from the city to the Nemetskaya Sloboda, the section where the foreigners in Moscow were compelled to live so as not to corrupt the pious Muscovites. These were a motley group of adventurers, traders, men of every nationality in Europe, and they looked at all the problems of the Kremlin with an eye to their own personal interests. Some found it to their advantage to support Prince Golitsyn as the leading champion of Western influence in the Russian capital and the mainstay of Sofia. Others held posts in Peter's new regiments, the Preobrazhensky and the Semenovsky, and these naturally sympathized with the Naryshkins. Yet with few exceptions, they thought only of themselves and their careers and were ready to take either side, if it promised them more wealth and promotion.

The only exceptions were those few men who were official or unofficial agents of the different European powers. Moscow did not care to indulge in formal diplomatic relations with the West but in the Nemetskaya Sloboda there were always secret agents of the chief European rulers. These men watched every move on the checkerboard of Muscovite politics and sought as well as they could to influence them. They were puzzled by the attitude of Mazeppa who seemed utterly guileless and innocent of the world around him. They could only attribute it to his trust and confidence in Golitsyn.

So while the Hetman was busied with his feasts and pleasures, skilful agents of all factions tried to sound out the members of his staff. They tried to sway them with promises and warnings. The Naryshkins kept hinting that if Peter came to power, there would be a new Hetman and that Mazeppa like his predecessor Samoylovych for real or imagined disloyalty to the Tsar would journey on to Siberia. They worked not only in Moscow but they sent agents to Kiev and the Hetman's capital of Baturyn to stir up ill feeling. Still others went to the Zaporozhian Sich to fan that spirit of unrest which had so often thwarted the hopes of the Kozaks for full independence and had exacted a heavy toll from the Ukrainian people.

Yet Mazeppa seemed to pay no attention. He was fully occupied with his good friend Golitsyn. As the official representative of the Zaporozhian Host on a state visit, he would not allow himself to be distracted. It was in vain that his most loyal friends and supporters warned him of the dangers around him. Hidden rivals for his position tried equally vainly to urge him to some move. They received the same courteous but unresponsive hearing.

Now and then, along with the couriers from Baturyn would come some nun with reports on the problems of the Kiev-Pechersky Convent of the Ascension, one of the largest of the Ukrainian convents. This was natural for only a few years before the Orthodox Church of Kiev had been placed under the jurisdiction of the Patriarch of Moscow and this had raised many troublesome and complicated questions. To settle these, the venerable Abbess, the Mother Mary Magdalen, had been forced to come to Moscow. She was now there. She was well over seventy years of age but time had dealt lightly with her. Her mind was still acute and that great political talent which she had had in the world stood her in good stead. She was in close contact with the Patriarch Joachim and the other leaders of the Church and of the Patriarchal court. Few, either of the Muscovites or Ukrainians, realized that the retiring nun was a person of importance and fewer realized that she was the mother of the Hetman of Ukraine. Yet such she was. After her husband's death, she had retired from the world and her rise in the religious life had been as startling as that of her son.

On August 5, this seemingly carefree life came to a sudden end. That evening there were rumors afloat. A secret order was issued to mobilize the streltsy. As the men grumblingly left their evening haunts, it was whispered almost openly that Sofia and Prince Golitsyn had decided to seize Peter and his mother and remove them from the capital to an unknown destination. Some one, probably not without the instructions of the Scotch general Patrick Gordon, Peter's most devoted associate, warned the young Tsar and Peter, leaping out of bed in his night-clothes, mounted a horse and galloped off to the Monastery of St. Serge some forty versts away. He reached it safely and he was soon joined there by his mother and his wife. His own regiments were ordered to follow him and in this relatively safe spot, behind the massive walls of the Monastery, Peter waited quietly.

The news came as a bombshell to Moscow. Sofia tried to persuade Peter to return to the capital. He refused. She tried threats. There was no result. Slowly at first and then in ever increasing numbers, prominent officials began to make their way to the monastery. As a last resort, Sofia asked the Patriarch to undertake the task of getting Peter back. He accepted the mission and remained at the Monastery. All persons, including the Abbess Mary Magdalen, who had necessary and pressing business with the Patriarch, had to visit him there.

Sofia soon realized that the balance of power had shifted and that her control of Moscow was nearing its end. In a few days it was a question of self-preservation. Prince Golitsyn suddenly realized that he had to visit his estates and he secretly left the capital, for he knew that Peter regarded him as one of his worst enemies. His departure was so sudden that he had no time to say farewell to Mazeppa and the Hetman was left in splendid isolation.

The days were an ever-increasing nightmare. From being a popular figure in the life of Moscow, Mazeppa found himself shunned as if he were a leper or a victim of some contagious disease. His friends disappeared from their accustomed haunts. A few endeavored to make peace with Peter and journeyed to the Monastery. Others went to their estates for their health. A steadily increasing number were arrested; their property was confiscated and they themselves were executed or started for Siberia. No one wanted to know the Hetman of Ukraine who was regarded as the very symbol of the Golitsyn regime.

Mazeppa realized the danger of his position. He could hardly hope to escape deposition and arrest. He thought of the fate of his predecessor, Samoylovych, who had been railroaded to Siberia to cover the military failure of Golitsyn and whose disgrace had led to his own advancement. Already the fires of ambition, fanned by the Naryshkins, were being lighted among his subordinates and more than one of the general officers and colonels in his retinue dreamed of receiving the coveted mace and the horsetail standard of the Hetman, not to speak of the vast wealth and power that went with the title.

Mazeppa alone seemed outwardly unperturbed. He listened to the pleadings of his officers to leave Moscow and said nothing. His friends and his would-be rivals united in urging him to return quietly to his capital at Baturyn without fanfare or publicity. They argued that there he might be able to ride out the storm and once the new regime was established, he might be able to attract the favorable attention of the new Tsar. There too he could quiet the unrest that was already springing up among the Kozaks, for rumors were spreading in Ukraine that the Hetman and his staff had been arrested and that it was necessary to choose a new Hetman.

Mazeppa listened with infinite patience to the advice given him and said nothing. He was sure of the motives of each of his officers and whether they were loyal or jealous but he gave no sign. That same enigmatic attitude toward friend and foe that had guided him to high position he maintained without a word.

He determined to risk everything by staying but he could not reveal his reasons to his closest friends, much less to the Muscovites. He did not look at the situation as a theoretical thinker. He was not one. He was a typical product of the scholastic education of his time and well trained in the school of practical politics.

He realized that if he left Moscow, his doom was sealed. He would definitely proclaim himself a partisan of Golitsyn. He would admit that he owed his position to the Muscovites and that he held it subject to their good pleasure and while he was willing to use that support to gain his post, he had too high an ideal of the post of Hetman to make a public demonstration of his practical dependence.

Besides, he was in Moscow on a formal visit to the Tsars and their government. That in his mind overshadowed the hospitality that he had received from Golitsyn and the Regent Sofia. He was there to meet Peter who had so far refused to see him. He had met Ivan and if the regime had changed and Peter was in control, there was so much more reason for him to remain until he did see him.

Furthermore he was the Hetman of the Zaporozhian Host and Ukraine. He knew that his predecessor Hetman Bohdan Khmelnytsky had signed in 1654 a Treaty with the representatives of the Tsar at the city of Pereyaslav. This had been in reality a military alliance but the use of certain phrases had allowed the Muscovites to claim a predominant position in the country and to interfere in the affairs of the Host. That treaty had been renewed by each succeeding Hetman and each time the liberties of the Host had been recognized in the treaty. Mazeppa was in his own mind not a subject but an ally of the Tsar and hence with his logical, if somewhat pedantic, way of thinking he should not outwardly concern himself with changes in the Muscovite regime. "The Tsar is dead. Long live the Tsar!" and it was his obligation to make sure that the new Tsar respected the rights of the Hetman and of the Zaporozhian Host. Of course he could not say this aloud. Many of his own officers did not accept the logic of his position and a word of this to the Muscovites who regarded the Treaty of Pereyaslav as the equivalent of full submission would have given new causes for complaint against him.

Besides, strange as it may seem, he felt himself safer at Moscow than at Baturyn. Even with his friends out of power, he had a wider acquaintance in Moscow than any of the other officers. The Naryshkin party was in a way disorganized by its sudden success. Sofia had seen to it that most of the more able members of the family had been liquidated in the revolt of the streltsy and the Moscow mob a few years before. Mazeppa had with him still large sums of money and valuables which he had brought to distribute as presents and if bribery was the thing to do, he was able to do it. He had with him many of the most ambitious officers and if he could not consult with his friends at Baturyn, neither could they and it was almost impossible for them to form a party against him, while he and they were in Moscow. Finally it was easier for him there to keep himself informed on events in the Monastery and be prepared to take action without delay when it became advisable. Even the Abbess Mary Magdalen was in the Monastery and she was not his only source of information.

All depended upon his remaining cool and collected and whatever fears or anxieties he might have had, he kept them to himself and with iron nerve he held to his apparently foolhardy course. And so it seemed. Already Prince Golitsyn and his wife had been arrested and were on their way to Siberia. All the wealth of that once powerful prince had been confiscated and in one step he had passed from being the second man in the realm to an ordinary convict.

Suddenly on September 10, after a month of suspense, Mazeppa felt the situation ripe for action. Perhaps he had been warned or perhaps it was his own sense of timing. At all events he announced that he was going to the Monastery to meet Peter. He could not be dissuaded.

With the same pomp and dignity with which he had entered
Moscow to meet Sofia and Golitsyn, Ivan Mazeppa and his party
started for the Monastery of St. Serge. Preceded by his horse-tail
standard, carrying his mace, and clad in all the regalia of his office,
Mazeppa and his brilliant group moved out through the gates of
Moscow and into the countryside. The population looked on in
amazement at this apparent act of bravado. Many a man in the
group and perhaps Mazeppa himself wondered if it was the last
ride before exile or execution, for Muscovite ruthlessness was pro-
verbial and the Naryshkins were giving a good demonstration of it.

The cavalcade reached the Monastery. There was not a sign
that it was expected and the Hetman simply sent in the message
that he wished to pay his respects to Tsar Peter. To the surprise
of all he was admitted with scarcely any delay. He was ushered
into the august presence and as time passed, both friends and
enemies wondered if Mazeppa would appear alive and free.

There was something fantastic about the interview. The
seventeen year old Tsar, nearly eight feet tall, was ungainly and
uncouth. His manners were those of the drunken carousers of the
Nemetskaya Sloboda, for if Peter spurned the rigid courtesy of
the old Muscovite tradition, he was equally contemptuous of the
finer aspects of Western courtly behavior. Opposite him was
Mazeppa, well past fifty years of age and a past master of French
and Polish courtesy and social graces. But with his life and his
position depending upon the outcome of this meeting, Mazeppa
set himself to win the Tsar's favor and he succeeded.

He undoubtedly had much to explain but he could boast of his
services to Moscow on the expeditions with Prince Golitsyn and he
undoubtedly put those services in the best possible light. Peter
had previously doubted the value and the success of Golitsyn's
schemes. Now the Hetman presented them in a new light and we
can be sure with no lack of emphasis on his own role. He told
the truth or what seemed to Peter to be the truth. He brought

out costly presents and gave them to the Tsar. He ran through the entire gamut of emotions and when he finished, Peter was convinced. Mazeppa had won his confidence. The Tsar confirmed him in all his rights and privileges; he also confirmed the rights and privileges of the Host. Peter did more; he ordered to be returned to Mazeppa all the gifts that he had made to Golitsyn and gave him a good slice of the exiled prince's property.

When Mazeppa finally left the Tsar and rejoined his officers, they could scarcely believe their own eyes. The miracle had happened. The opposition and the intrigues among his staff were over and as the little band rode back to Moscow, Ivan Mazeppa was more truly than ever the Hetman of Ukraine.

Perhaps he had been helped by a curious incident. In 1686 King Jan Sobieski of Poland had made an alliance with Moscow against Turkey. Now with Sofia and Golitsyn out of the way and with Peter still young and untried, he conceived the idea of bringing Ukraine back under the Polish crown. The Polish King thought that Mazeppa's insecurity as Hetman might lead him to shift his allegiance to save his own head. So a French agent in Moscow, de Neuville, disguised as a Russian, and a German doctor then in the capital approached the Hetman to secure his cooperation. Mazeppa flatly refused to listen to the suggestion. It showed how thoroughly the Poles misunderstood. He remembered too well his earlier relations at the Polish court and he knew that the King could not carry out his promises to the Kozaks against the wish of the magnates who were intent upon plundering and subduing the Kozaks in every way possible. The offer was no temptation to Mazeppa. But it gave him another argument to prove his loyalty to Peter and to show that he was concerned about the relations of Ukraine to Moscow and was not a partisan of any faction in the land of the Tsars.

On September 12, Mazeppa and his party started on their return to Baturyn. They were escorted out of Moscow with the same formality that had greeted them on their arrival. There had been a revolution in Moscow and Mazeppa had weathered it. He was still Hetman. He had protected the position of the Host and he had emerged more powerful than before. The rumors that had been spread throughout Ukraine by his enemies were silenced by his reappearance. The malcontents in Kiev and Baturyn vanished and even those members of the Sich who had hoped to profit by a period of unrest and confusion almost universally relapsed into a sullen silence.

CHAPTER TWO

THE KOZAKS AND THE ZAPOROZHIAN HOST

Mazeppa had left Moscow as Hetman and not as a prisoner on his way to Siberia or execution and he had escaped the fate of his Russian friends. Yet, the dangerous situation in which he had found himself could not leave him unaware of the limitations that were imposed upon him and his people by their relations with the Tsar of Moscow. At the same time the glowing promises of the Polish King in their turn emphasized the importance of the Zaporozhian Host in the tangled politics of the day and stressed the power of that organization of which he was the master.

The Zaporozhian Host was an anomaly in the Europe of the seventeenth century but it had developed in response to a real need. There was nothing artificial about it. It was the mouthpiece of the Ukrainian people and it reflected their individuality, their love of liberty and their stubborn adherence to their own traditions and culture.

It was the natural continuation of the once great state of Kievan Rus, the first state of the Ukrainian people. It was at Kiev in 998 that the Grand Prince Volodymyr, better known by his Church Slavic name of St. Vladimir, had formally accepted Eastern Christianity from Constantinople and had married the daughter of the Byzantine Emperor. The dynasty was connected by marriage with all the reigning houses of Europe. Yaroslav the Wise, the son of Volodymyr, had arranged the marriage of one of his daughters to the King of France and there were matrimonial connections with the rulers of Poland, Hungary, Scandinavia and the Holy Roman Empire. Later another Grand Prince, Volodymyr Monomakh, married a daughter of Harold, the last Saxon ruler of England. Moscow had not been founded and with its wealth, luxury and power, Kiev was the richest daughter of Constantinople and the inheritor of its cultural traditions. Prince Alexis K. Tolstoy was not exaggerating when he wrote:

> When Germany lay sunk in gloom and darkness,
> In Kiev there were more than forty schools.

Then evil times came upon the land. Civil wars broke out among the princes. In 1169 Prince Andrey Bogolyubsky of Suzdal, one of the descendants of Monomakh, attacked and sacked Kiev and transferred all the signs of power to his northern capital from which they passed to Moscow. Invading hordes of Asiatic nomads cut the territory of Kievan Rus off from the Black Sea. Finally in 1240 the great invasion of the Mongols decimated the population and ruined the cities. Moscow submitted to these invaders and became more Asiatic than the Asiatics. Kiev tried to resist and in the unequal struggle fell under the control of Lithuania and later passed into the Polish Republic. Independent Ukraine had ceased to exist.

Political activity almost completely stopped. Life, traditions and culture lived on. But with the fall of Constantinople to the Turks in 1453, those streams of learning that had come from the imperial capital on the Bosphorus dried up. At the same time in the sixteenth century the Renaissance had awakened the Poles to a more active cultural life. The Ukrainian lords slowly but with increasing speed drifted away from their old culture and traditions and became submerged in the Polish current. Many abandoned their Orthodox Church for the Roman Catholic Church, the Church of the Poles, or became Uniats, Catholics acknowledging the Papacy but maintaining the Eastern Rite and culture of their ancestors. By the end of the sixteenth century, the Ukrainian cause seemed lost and only the Orthodox Church Brotherhoods in some of the cities were struggling to revive and reanimate the popular spirit.

Then the Kozaks developed. The fertile but uncultivated steppes of Ukraine were constantly ravaged by bands of nomadic Tatars who after the breakup of the Mongol Empire established their own khanate in the Crimea. In the sixteenth century bold and daring men went out into the steppes from the settled areas of Ukraine to hunt and fish. Grouped in bands, they were able to defy the Tatars and to guard the frontiers of the settled regions. These men took the name of Kozaks and they were stirred by the same impulses that led the Spanish conquistadores to the New World and inspired the English sailors to push out into the Atlantic Ocean to singe the beard of the King of Spain and to bring back to England the fabulous wealth that the Spaniards had garnered in the Indies.

The Kozaks increased in numbers and in wealth. For greater protection and security they established their own fort below the rapids of the Dnieper and this developed into the celebrated Zaporozhian Sich.[1] The military fame of the Kozaks spread throughout Europe and the Kozak troops came to form an important part of the Polish army. They were in a sense hard-fighting irregular troops well trained for specialized warfare against the highly mobile Tatars. They extended their activities further and in their light boats they ravaged all the ports of the Turkish Empire and even dared to burn the suburbs of Constantinople itself. They were fanatically Orthodox and the bitter enemies of both the Roman Catholic Poles whom they acknowledged as sovereigns and the Mohammedan Turks and Tatars. Thousands of Christian girls seized by the nomads and destined for the harems of the great Turkish nobles were set free by these Kozak raids and thousands of men destined to become galley slaves were liberated.

Yet this great movement of the Kozaks had one glaring weakness. The Kozaks were far more interested in liberty and fighting than in political organization and administration. They remained a military force of uncertain loyalty. The Sich was a man's institution. When an individual went to it, he left his wife and children in their native village under Polish control, while he accepted the democratic system of the Sich.

There the Kozaks revelled and feasted and acknowledged no law but their own whims. Yet when they started on some raid or expedition, whether by land or sea, they selected a Hetman to command them and practiced and enforced a strict military discipline.

---

1 Zaporozhe—beyond the rapids.

The Hetman's word was law, but when the campaign was over, he could be judged by the men of the Sich as to his success or non-success and be rewarded or punished accordingly.

The Zaporozhian Host, as the men of the Sich called themselves, was a curious combination of an army and a religious brotherhood. It had remarkable similarities to the great military orders of the Crusades and the men often referred to themselves as knights. The Host became the spokesman for the Ukrainian people who were suffering under Polish domination. It voiced their aspirations and their love of freedom and was in fact their only means of expression. Yet by the very nature of the Sich, it made no effort to send up a government for them or to clarify their position or its own. Here was the root of the troubles of the later Hetmans.

Nominally Polish subjects, the Kozaks became both the strongest part of the Polish state and the greatest menace to it. They were given almost complete liberty in their undertakings and broad grants of legal exemptions. They were thus in a way an independent army in a feudally organized state. When the King of Poland was at war with either the Turks or the Tatars, the Kozaks of the Sich were valuable allies and their numbers grew rapidly as volunteers streamed in. When the King sought peace, the Kozaks continued their raids and he was showered with protests from the Sultan of Turkey, the Khan of the Crimea and the Tsar of Moscow. Under these protests he tried to reduce their numbers and to force many back into practical serfdom. He was powerless to control them or to guide their actions. They did not fit into the Polish system nor were they outside it.

Then the Kings of Poland tried a curious compromise. They formally registered a few thousand Kozaks and tried to make these a regular and reliable force. They recognized Kozak officers in different parts of their Ukrainian territories and gave them a permanent status. These officers were selected from the more wealthy and influential Kozaks but they soon came to form a Kozak upper class with special rights and perquisites. They controlled the finances of the various Kozak regiments and their personal fortunes and those of their regiments became inextricably confused. At the same time the old unordered life went on at the Sich and more and more there came an unofficial gap between this and the regiments with the Sich still maintaining its old claims to the control of the Kozak movement.

It was obviously not a happy solution. Poland was in a sad political condition, for the great magnates were becoming steadily more unruly and able to thwart all the actions of the King. The King never had the money to pay the sums promised to the registered Kozaks but on the outbreak of any war, he asked the officers to increase their forces and in peace times to reduce them again. The magnates for their part treated the Orthodox Kozak officers as little better than pariahs and outlaws.

The Polish course was obvious. The government had to effect a proper compromise with the Kozak organization and incorporate it into the state or to suppress it. The King favored the first policy. The magnates chose the second but they refused to undertake the task of doing it. They preferred pinpricks and insults to the stern task of suppressing this turbulent military force. The result was a long series of violent outbreaks alternating with equally ruthless attempts at suppression.

The climax came in 1648 when Bohdan Khmelnytsky as Hetman raised the standard of revolt. This became the most bloody and violent of all the Kozak movements. Bohdan proved himself an able leader and after he had won a series of sweeping victories in alliance with the Khan of the Crimea, he undertook to set up an independent Kozak state. He expelled the Polish landlords and administrators and replaced them with Ukrainians. For a while he dreamed of an alliance with Moldavia and Wallachia, semi-autonomous Orthodox states in the Ottoman Empire. As a result Ukraine reappeared on the map of Europe as the independent land of the Zaporozhian Host with Bohdan as its ruler.

With the King's officials and wojewodas out of the way, Bohdan had to create a new system of administration and he turned to the one organized group at hand, the colonels of the various local regiments. These soon became not only the military but the civilian heads of the larger districts and their captains or sotnyks took over the distinctively local control. This combination of the military and civilian forces at all levels in the state of almost constant warfare against Poland made the civilian administration very difficult, for the colonels were constantly called into the field to the detriment of their administrative duties.

Bohdan was not able to strengthen his country sufficiently to have it stand alone and in an evil hour in 1654 by the Treaty of Pereyaslav, he placed the Zaporozhian Host under the nominal protection of Tsar Alexis of Moscow and made a military alliance with him. In return the Tsar's representatives promised to preserve all the rights and privileges of the Host and to protect it against Poland. Relations were carried on through the Muscovite foreign office as if Ukraine were a separate state. Part of the Kozak officers questioned the wisdom of Bohdan's actions for they realized that the Muscovite autocratic system would be unacceptable to the freedom-loving Kozaks. They were overruled by the rank and file of the Host who in their fanaticism against the Catholic Poles saw only that the Muscovites were Orthodox like themselves. They did not even think of the differences in temperament and administration and were enthusiastic about the Treaty.

Once the Treaty was signed, the Tsar did not delay in breaking it and attempting to place the Ukrainians under the iron rule of Moscow. He placed garrisons in several of the Ukrainian cities on the excuse of protecting the Kozaks from the Poles and these soon began to interfere in the internal administration of the Host.

For about one year, despite the steady encroachments of the Muscovites in violation of the Treaty of Pereyaslav, it seemed as if the troubles with Poland had reached a definite end. During 1655 a new coalition was formed against that country by Moscow and Ukraine. Then the other neighbors of Poland, Brandenburg and some of the princes of Moldavia, Wallachia and Transylvania joined it. But the heart of the opposition to Poland was Charles X Gustav of Sweden.

The action of Sweden was of great importance to Ukraine, for at that period Sweden, which already held Finland and a large section south of the Gulf of Finland, was definitely trying to make the Baltic Sea a Swedish lake. To do this the Vasa Kings of Sweden reasserted their right to the Polish throne.

At the end of the sixteenth century King John III of Sweden had married a Polish princess and his son Zygmunt, the father of Jan Kazimierz, was the legitimate heir to the thrones of both Sweden and Poland. Yet it proved impossible for him to hold both countries. Zygmunt was an ardent Catholic and by this time Sweden had accepted Lutheranism and refused to recognize a Catholic King. The Swedes accepted as King Charles IX, a member of the Lutheran branch of the Vasa family, while the Poles supported the Catholic branch. This started a series of wars which lasted for more than a half century as each king tried to gain the crown of his relative. The Swedish family gained ground at the expense of the Polish and in 1655 it almost seemed as if it would be able to take what it wished of Poland and leave the rest to Ukraine and the other neighbors.

In 1656 the Swedes, Ukrainians and Muscovites actually held most of Poland and King Jan Kazimierz was even compelled to flee to Silesia.

Khmelnytsky saw in this Swedish advance the hope of disentangling himself from his alliance with Moscow and he signed a treaty with Sweden, when he saw that Moscow would not allow any territory conquered from Poland in the north to be taken over by Ukraine.

This was not to be for the Poles unexpectedly rallied and with the support of the Emperor in Vienna, the Swedes were forced to retire and Jan Kazimierz came back to his throne.

It was just at this period in 1657 that Bohdan Khmelnytsky died. He had been failing for some time. He tried to place his young and weak son Yuri in his place as Hetman but Yuri was unable to maintain himself and the unity of the Host was split. There grew up a Polish faction consisting chiefly of the officers who

sought some compromise with Poland in return for a guarantee of
liberties. The Muscovite group, numerically the larger and repre-
senting the rank and file, opposed this in the name of the Orthodox
religion. At the same time they resented the slowly developing
Ukrainian political system and yet they equally resented every sign
of Muscovite domination on Ukrainian territory.

Factionalism degenerated into open civil war as both Muscovite
and Polish leaders fanned the flames of discord. This was embittered by open war between Moscow and Poland on Ukrainian
territory. Then in 1667 Moscow and Poland signed a treaty of peace
and divided Ukraine between them along the line of the Dnieper
River with Kiev on the western bank being handed over to Moscow.
The resulting chaos and devastation ushered in that sad period
graphically termed by Ukrainian historians the Ruin.

Ukraine was hopelessly split and the Hetman was in no position
to exercise his power on the two banks. It became necessary to have
two Hetmans, one for the Polish section and one for the Muscovite.
Once this was done, it was child's play for the two powers to keep
the Hetmans from agreeing and adopting a common policy. The
Polish landlords were able to recover their estates, resume their
control and abrogate most of the privileges previously won by the
Kozaks. In the east Moscow was likewise able to force the Hetmans
to carry out its policy without regard to the feelings of the Ukrainian
population.

At the same time discord started between the Sich and the
Kozak regiments. The Sich had definitely ceased to be the centre
of Kozak authority. Its members still continued their raiding
and their more or less non-political activity but no one took seriously
their claims to control the naming of the Hetmans on either bank.
The refusal of the Sich to recognize the new situation isolated it from
the general developments of the Ukrainian life and added to the
troubles of the Hetmans.

This was the situation when Ivan Mazeppa began to play his
role in Kozak affairs.

CHAPTER THREE

THE EARLY LIFE OF MAZEPPA

There are many questions still unanswered as to the early life and family of Ivan Mazeppa but we know enough from the definite statements and documents of his contemporaries and from general pictures of the life of the period to answer most of them with strong probability and it requires very little imagination to place him and his family within the general framework of the period.

The family of the future Hetman was one of the prominent Ukrainian noble families in the neighborhood of Bila Tserkva in the province of Kiev. We can trace it back to the middle of the sixteenth century when in 1544 King Zygmunt I of Poland gave to one Mykola Mazeppa-Kolodynsky the estate of Mazepyntsi in this area and thereby rendered him liable for service in the cavalry. His son Mykhaylo received in 1572 a renewed confirmation of this grant from King Zygmunt Avgust and two years later Henry of Valois, during his short tenure of the Polish crown, gave him also the village of Pisochna near Lyubomyr. This made the family prominent and wealthy.

Mykhaylo seems to have left two children, Teodor and Mykola. Teodor was active in the Kozak disturbances of the end of the century and for taking part in the uprising of Kosynsky, Loboda and Nalyvayko he was condemned to death in Warsaw in 1597. Some of the Ukrainian chronicles of the period refer to him as a colonel. His brother Mykola apparently was not involved but remained quietly on his estate of Mazepyntsi which he held as a fief and which was again subjected to litigation during an examination of the legality of its ownership.

The next Mazeppa of whom we hear was Adam Stepan and he was probably the father of Ivan. A curious story about him well illustrates the general conditions in Poland in the early part of the seventeenth century. In a fit of anger, he drew his sword and killed a young Polish nobleman, Zielinski. For this he was summoned to court but sure of his own position he declined to appear and was accordingly condemned *in absentia* to be disgraced and executed. Adam Mazeppa paid no more attention, even when a royal order demanded the confiscation of his estates. There was a considerable amount of legal manoeuvering but he finally received a full pardon, apparently by becoming reconciled with the family of the man whom he had killed. We have no idea whether he had appealed to the King in person or had succeeded either through personal charm or through the use of money in securing this change of judgment. It is equally possible that King Zygmunt Vasa took the position that in view of the Kozak unrest in the neighborhood of Bila Tserkva, it would be a wise measure to pardon a Kozak of a noble family and thus try to secure another adherent of the Polish crown. It is also not excluded in accordance with the religious disturbances of the time that Adam embraced or seemed to embrace the Catholic faith as the way out of his difficulties. Whatever the situation it did not affect his standing in the community and gave him a certain glamor among the Kozak officers.

Apparently during Khmelnytsky's struggle to free Ukraine he was the Ottoman of the Bila Tserkva regiment. Yet fundamentally, although as Stepan he signed the Treaty of Pereyaslav, he did not break his relations with the Poles. He supported the efforts of Hetman Vyhovsky to bring Ukraine back to the Polish Republic as a third co-equal partner with Poland and Lithuania as provided by the Treaty of Hadyach. When this failed in 1659 King Jan Kazimierz again confirmed his title to Mazepyntsi and changed it from a fief to a manor and in 1662 gave him the honorary title of Chernyhiv cup-bearer.

We are on surer ground with regard to Ivan's mother. She was Maryna Mokiyevska, a member of another Ukrainian gentry family from the general neighborhood. She was an extremely well educated and intelligent lady and was trained in the Florovo-Ascension Convent in Kiev which was the leading educational institution for Orthodox Ukrainian girls of good families. She was rigorously

Orthodox at a time when the Ukrainian gentry were becoming Polonized and Catholic in large numbers. Far from following the fashionable trend, she joined the Orthodox Brotherhood of Lutsk, one of those organizations which were endeavoring to revive the Ukrainian national and religious spirit. We do not know the exact date of her birth but as she died over 90 in 1707 as the Abbess Mary Magdalen, she could scarcely have been born after 1610. After her husband's death, she retired from the world and became a nun in the same convent in which she had been educated and very soon became the Abbess there and was in charge also of a convent in the city of Hlukhiv. Everything speaks of her superior ability in both religious and secular affairs and we know in considerable detail of the influence which she exerted upon her brilliant son.

The date of her marriage is likewise unknown and this helps to create the uncertainty as to the birthday of Ivan. He must have been born sometime between 1629 and 1642, although the date has been pushed as early as 1622 but this seems somewhat extreme. At the present time in the lack of direct evidence, Ukrainian scholars have come to regard his birth date as March 20, 1632, although Mazeppa never gave any direct hints as to his correct age. He was well preserved, even at an advanced age and at the time of the battle of Poltava in 1709, European diplomats who knew him personally placed him as between sixty five and eighty, a wide enough margin to satisfy all objectors to any given date.

Ivan had one sister, Oleksandra. Her birthdate is also uncertain but she was probably younger than he and perhaps considerably so, for she married for the first time in 1674 and her first son Jan Obidowski was born in 1676.

Yet if the ravages of time and war have destroyed the definite data as to the precise age of the family, there is abundant evidence that they formed an especially close-knit family group and that the mother was the dominant personality. She continually both as a woman of the world and as a nun was intensely interested in the career of her children upon whom she had a decisive influence.

Ivan respected her and again and again turned to her for advice. He was equally devoted to his sister and never lost an opportunity to assist her and fashion proper careers for her children. Oleksandra, however, does not seem to have been a strong and dominant character and her life was scarcely one of unalloyed satisfaction.

There also can be no doubt as to the form of life in which the future Hetman was reared. From his earliest days he lived on a large estate in one of the most charming locations on the right bank of the Dnieper. In the manor house good taste and formalism were the dominant qualities. It was the life of the higher type of Kozak officers and of the Polish gentry of the day and the native traditions were harmoniously blended with the new culture that had been introduced from the West.

As soon as the boy was old enough to sit in the saddle, he was taught to ride, to shoot and to hunt and as he grew older, there was an abundance of larger and more dangerous game to test his courage and his skill. In addition he was brought up in the atmosphere of the Kozak officer class. There were the military exercises carried on by the Bila Tserkva regiment and in times of peace these gatherings became occasions for unlimited hospitality. Both his father and the Kozak officers who were his guests could tell many and endless tales of Kozak heroism under the most dangerous situations and amid the feasting and merriment the children could not fail to overhear stories which would make them dream also of further adventures which they would undertake themselves.

Life was almost ideal for the children. Their parents were busy with their own pleasures and duties. Discipline was easy and far too often study was more honored in the breach than the observance. There was an abundance of servants constantly on duty and everything was done to make the future master of the house conscious of his own importance and of the rule which he was soon to fill in the neighborhood and the district.

Then too there was the colorful life of the peasants. Every event of the year was marked by entertainments and pageantry.

There were celebrations and complicated folk rites at Christmas, Easter, and St. John's Eve, the Summer Solstice with its manifold bonfires. Seedtime and harvest, winter and spring, summer and autumn, all had their traditional usages which were practiced in the manor house as well as in the peasant cottage and each of these brought large numbers of invited and uninvited guests.

The estates were largely self-contained and on the whole they were prosperous. There was no lack of money and little need for it for almost everything except some imported articles of luxury were raised on the estate and stored away in the many barns and storehouses.

The Mazeppas were friends and relatives of all the landowning families of the district, whether they considered themselves Poles or Kozaks, and as he grew older, the young Ivan was a welcome guest at household after household where the young people gathered in an unceasing round of dances, pleasure and entertainment.

Politics was the one subject of conversation. There was always something happening, some new gossip from Warsaw or from Grodno where the Polish Diet met. There was something to report from the local diets, some new threat of confederations among the Poles to affect the position of the King, some new political combinations that aroused the interests pro and con of all the families in the district. Religion was second in importance and despite the bitter fanaticism that existed among the peasants and the rank and file of the Kozaks, the Kozak officers though Orthodox were good friends of their Polish Catholic neighbors, except when some popular outbreak or tactless act of the government served to kindle the flames of religious bigotry.

Mazeppa then passed his early years in an atmosphere of serenity and magnificence, where pleasure seemed the chief end of life and where few or none pondered deeply on ethical and moral questions which seemed far less interesting and important than questions of faith and ritual. Courtesy and elegance were the virtues of the day. Compliments and flattery were the natural accompaniments of all social relations and the goal of the young man was to become a courtier.

There was also a coarser and sterner side for when aroused to sudden anger, these nobles knew no law but their own will. It was very easy to resent an insult by drawing the sword and although most of these episodes were quietly settled by the friends present, they not infrequently became serious and broke up sometimes for years old friendships and almost precipitated private wars.

We can be sure that the tone of the Mazeppa household was set by the mother and that she with her deep sense of religion and her good education saw to it that pleasure and frivolity were not allowed to get out of bounds and to crowd out the more serious business of life. She undoubtedly saw to it that her son learned to read and write from the parish priest who at this period in Ukraine had usually received considerable education, particularly if he were to serve near a cultured manor house. It was probably in his early years that Mazeppa learned to read and write both Polish and that curious written language, a mixture of Ukrainian and Church Slavic, that was the written language of the educated Ukrainians of the day.

When it came time for his further education, Mazeppa was sent to Kiev. He probably entered the Kiev Brotherhood School for his first formal training and from there he went on to the Kievo-Mohylanska College, the finest educational institution of the Orthodox Church not only in Ukraine but in the whole of Eastern Europe. This had been established by the Metropolitan Petro Mohyla to offer under Orthodox auspices and in an Orthodox atmosphere that training which was being given by the Jesuit Colleges which were springing up all over Poland.

Its curriculum was very narrow. The students studied Church Slavic in its Ukrainian form, Polish and Latin. They devoted wearisome hours to those courses in rhetoric and philosophy which were the rule in Poland and which had long been outmoded in Western Europe. They took part in religious disputations and in the preparation of what passed for drama but they were not encouraged to pay much attention to modern history or to familiarize themselves with the achievements of the West during the current century. Indeed with the Thirty Years War still being waged, Poland and Ukraine were in a kind of cultural and political backwater which behind the embittered fury of the religious wars in Germany had given them a chance to put their own affairs in order, an opportunity which they sadly neglected.

This education had a great effect upon Mazeppa. He became an excellent Latin scholar. He could deliver a eulogy or a good oration in fluent Latin; he could turn a gracious compliment in several languages. As a result of his later studies, he added to this at least a speaking knowledge of German, Italian, French and Dutch. He could take real pleasure in listening to the florid panegyrics which were the staple products of the College whenever it welcomed distinguished guests. In a word Mazeppa absorbed that artificial culture which was the dominant force in the Poland of the day and which was in such strong contrast to the dour and uninspired culture of Moscow. It is small wonder that some later scholars came to believe that he had studied in a Jesuit institution either in Polotsk or Warsaw.

Yet despite his ease in quoting Plutarch, Cicero, Livy and Tacitus in season and out of season, we must not think of his stay in the Academy as one of work exclusively. Life in Kiev as the largest city of Ukraine with its many mementoes of the older and more recent past proved far more agreeable to a young man of Mazeppa's type than the lectures in the Academy. With the sons of other Kozak officers, he took part again in an endless round of gaiety and enjoyed himself to the full.

It is difficult to date the period of Mazeppa's study in Kiev or elsewhere. They must have included the years during which Hetman Khmelnytsky was carrying on the war for the liberation of Ukraine from Polish rule. There was fierce fighting around his home at Bila Tserkva. We know that his father during these eventful and bloody days was involved in the efforts of the Hetman and was one of the signers of the Treaty of Pereyaslav; yet there is nowhere any hint that Ivan was involved in it in any capacity either on the Ukrainian or the Polish side. It seems unusual that he could have remained uncommitted, occupied with his studies at Kiev at the very moment when Ukraine was so convulsed with war and revolution and when passions were roused to fever heat. Perhaps his family exerted pressure on him to remain at his studies. The Mazeppas were apparently one of those Ukrainian families which did not break off despite their patriotism all relations with their Polish neighbors and friends. Perhaps his relatives instinctively disapproved of the excesses of some of the peasant units which Khmelnytsky was unable to control. It is a troublesome problem and one that was never apparently noticed by his contemporaries, whether friends or enemies, or which for some reason they did not raise.

All we can say is that as quiet came back, we find Ivan Mazeppa on friendly terms with King Jan Kazimierz who trusted him and some time later sent him as one of a group of young nobles, both Polish and Ukrainian, to Western Europe. He seems to have been abroad for some three years. He was in France and studied for a while in the Sorbonne in Paris. He got to know and appreciate the spirit of France and of French art and life, especially in some of its lighter and perhaps less enviable aspects. Then he was given a special mission to study the manufacture and use of artillery in Holland and he was there for some time. He seems to have been also in Germany and it was probably on this journey, the equivalent of the Grand Tour as it was known later in Western Europe, that he picked up his knowledge of Italian. All we can say is that Ivan Mazeppa returned a little before 1659 from this journey and when he came back, he was already a grown and mature man able and ready to play his part in the political life of the day. His childhood and adolescence were over and from this moment we can begin with slight periods of uncertainty to trace his career as he rose to be the Hetman of Ukraine. It was a long, hard and confused climb but he is never far out of our sight and we can watch him as his political policy and skill developed.

CHAPTER FOUR

THE POLISH COURTIER

When Yuri Khmelnytsky failed to retain his control of the Host after his father's death, the officers turned to Ivan Vyhovsky and named him the new Hetman. It seemed a rational choice for Vyhovsky had been for years the secretary and the foreign minister of Bohdan. He had been familiar with all the plans of his former chief and he seemed the one man who might be able to carry through Bohdan's plans and through an alliance with Sweden rid himself of the Moscow stranglehold on the country. At first all seemed well but Vyhovsky who had never been known for his Muscophile affiliations did not reckon with the intrigues of the Tsar.

Moscow began to intrigue against him with some of the colonels on the east bank of the Dnieper and also with the ever turbulent officers of the Sich. When Sweden finally opened peace negotiations with Moscow and Poland, Vyhovsky realized that he had to make a counter-stroke.

He found but one immediately available, a complete reversal of his former policy and the conclusion of a new treaty with the King of Poland. In September, 1658 he and his representatives threw off the mask and in the Union of Hadyach, he arranged for the Host and Ukraine to re-enter the Polish Republic as the Grand Principality of Rus, a third independent member of that body on a par with Poland proper and Lithuania. He won almost all his conditions including the recognition of the Orthodox Church as the religion of Rus-Ukraine. In this agreement he had returned to the old Kozak policy as favored by the Polish Kings but he did not reckon with the whims of the magnates to whom everything Kozak and Orthodox was anathema and treason to the Polish Republic. Likewise he misjudged the hatred that the mass of the ordinary Kozaks had for Poland even without Muscovite instigation.

His ideas were supported by the higher officers and apparently with considerable enthusiasm by Adam Mazeppa, who by 1659 was already asking King Jan Kazimierz to confirm again his titles to his lands in Bila Tserkva. Here was a good opportunity for the young Ivan who had already been sent by the King to study abroad. Whatever doubt we may have had about Ivan's earlier movements, it now seems clear that he was back in the Polish court and in the favor of the King.

It seems very likely that Ivan Mazeppa was one of the Polish-Ukrainian representatives that appeared in Hadyach for the conclusion of the treaty that was to swing the Zaporozhian Host definitely away from the Muscovite autocracy and admit it to a free union with the Polish Republic.

If that was his hope and it seems that he was sincerely impressed by the King as well as by Vyhovsky, he was destined to be disappointed. At the meeting with the Kozaks he could not have failed to note the rising hostility against Vyhovsky on the part of the rank and file of the Kozaks and this became so marked that in September, 1659, just one year after his diplomatic success, Vyhovsky was compelled to lay down his post as Hetman and flee from a general meeting of the Host.

This was not the only disappointment in his efforts to produce peace and harmony. He could not fail to note that the agreement was equally detested by the Poles of those circles in which he moved, for the Polish nobles under threats of an armed confederation and an ensuing civil war forced the King to give up his hopes of having the Union accepted by the Diet. Some of these nobles had a personal grouch because Khmelnytsky had expelled them from their estates in Ukraine but the majority were actuated by a religious bigotry no more intelligent or far-sighted than that which had moved the Kozaks to turn on Vyhovsky and paid no attention to the obvious gains to both Poland and Ukraine through the new rapprochement.

Out of this disillusioning situation came an event that was to affect Mazeppa's fame in world literature. At some point on his return to the King in Grodno, Mazeppa fell in with a group of high Polish nobles, including one Jan Chrysostom Passek. With the customary lack of restraint that was then all too frequent, Passek and his friends were openly boasting that they would form a confederation against the King, if he did not denounce the agreement with the Kozaks. Mazeppa overheard this.

The young courtier was deeply shocked at such open disrespect and when he reached the King at Grodno where a general Diet was to meet, he revealed the conspiracy. The King thanked him and ordered the arrest of Passek and his crowd. Then the wheels of politics began to revolve. The Polish nobles came to the rescue of Passek and it was not long before the turbulent young nobleman received a full pardon and a liberal gift of money to atone for the charges that had been made against him. It should have been a warning to Mazeppa.

Some months later apparently at court, he met Passek again. In the meanwhile the Pole had vowed vengeance against him and whether drunk or not, he flared out at Mazeppa and called him Pan Osaul (Mr. Captain), apparently Ivan's rank in the Bila Tserkva regiment. Not to be outdone Mazeppa retorted with Pan Kapral (Mr. Corporal). Passek drew his sword and so did Mazeppa. A clash seemed imminent but the bystanders succeeded in averting it. However, since the King was in residence, the clash was treated as a serious offence and both young men were placed under arrest—not a serious punishment but one that was more insulting to their personal dignity than to their political standing. It could easily have led to a new outbreak between the Polish nobles and the Kozaks. The King wanted to avoid this and in a few days he pardoned the two on the ground of their youth, enthusiasm and ignorance of court routine and court courtesy. Mazeppa may have temporarily lost the favor of the King but it was not for long, for we soon find him engaged on other responsible missions to the Kozak officers.

After the forced withdrawal of Vyhovsky, the pro-Muscovite faction reelected as Hetman Yuri Khmelnytsky and formally repudiated the Union of Hadyach. This was only another interlude, for to secure his post Yuri had to resign the articles of alliance with the Tsar. These included significant limitations on the rights of the Kozaks who promised not to change Hetmans without the Tsar's consent and to allow an increase of the Muscovite garrisons in the Ukrainian cities, to pay Muscovite taxes and to give up independent diplomatic negotiations with foreign countries.

This was too much for the Kozaks and they forced Yuri to break off his relations with the Tsar and resume them with the King of Poland. The third force or rather the fourth, the Crimean Tatars, playing their usual double policy to check the rising power of the Host, also turned against Poland but when in 1660 Sheremetev at the head of a Muscovite army invaded Ukraine, Yuri joined the King and the two forced Sheremetev to surrender. As the price of his release, he turned over to the Tatars all the Kozaks who had sided with the Muscovite army and they were sold into slavery. Naturally this did not increase the popularity of Yuri and while the King offered a new agreement of autonomy to the Kozaks, he did not repeat the offer to have the Host reenter Poland as the Grand Principality of Rus. Jan Kazimierz, freed from his fear of Sweden, was going to stand out for stiffer terms.

The King preferred to make his own arrangements and to reward his friends. In 1662 he appointed Adam Mazeppa hereditary cup-bearer for Volyn and continued his favor to Ivan.

He again sent Ivan in February, 1663 to Yuri Khmelnytsky but again it was too little and too late, for Yuri had given up the struggle and retired to a monastery. He was succeeded by his brother-in-law, Colonel Pavel Teterya of the Pereyaslav Regiment. Teterya, while he received the King's letters, wrote back the almost insulting answer "Pan Mazeppa, a nobleman of your Royal Highness, can tell you much about the crimes and has heard the weeping and groaning of the inhabitants of Ukraine and was touched with sorrow. I have given him more detailed reports that are in line with his obligations—evidence of what he has seen with his own eyes and heard with his own ears."

Thus Mazeppa was brought face to face with the autocratic conduct of the Polish lords towards the Ukrainians on their estates, the abuses that had caused the revolt of Khmelnytsky and were now being revived as the Polish nobles recovered their lands because of the weakness and discord in the Kozak Host.

The King seems to have been satisfied with the conduct of Mazeppa, for on hearing of the new change of Hetmans, he sent Ivan back with the insignia to enthrone the Hetman and the appropriate credentials for himself. The choice may have been unwise for at the same time he had a letter from the King to Teterya asking him to protect the lands of Adam Mazeppa. Teterya refused to accept this embassy and called Mazeppa in his reply a "young cub." This may well have been because Teterya who was obviously a member of a different faction from Adam Mazeppa wanted a Polish magnate as an envoy and not a Kozak.

At the same time across the Dnieper Teterya's power was running out. It was challenged by various colonels and also by the leaders of the Sich. Mazeppa's letters apparently gave him the right to cross the Dnieper, if he found it wise and even to visit the Sich. He apparently regarded it better not to do it, for he returned to the King.

Yet by now Mazeppa was learning his lesson. Teterya and the other Kozaks had impressed upon him that there was no future for him in the Polish camp and the Poles had taught him the same lesson. He might have been sent to study in the West but he had received no missions except to the Kozaks and at every move, the Polish nobles had impressed upon him their opinion of a Kozak in the Polish service. He could never be accepted as eligible for any of the higher and more honorable posts.

Mazeppa's task was to disentangle himself from his Polish connections without losing the favor of the King. Chance came to his assistance. That same summer Teterya perhaps through other agents persuaded the King to cross with him to the East Bank to support him against Ivan Byrukhovetsky, the head of the Sich whom the Muscovites were supporting for Hetman. It can well be imagined that Ivan Mazeppa had no taste for precipitating a civil war in Ukraine to please either the Poles or the Muscovites. Ukraine needed peace and order.

On the way the expedition passed near Bila Tserkva and on one excuse or another Mazeppa found the occasion to retire to his estates. Possibly his father was failing in health and he used this as an excuse. Adam Mazeppa died sometime before 1665 and in that year the King formally appointed the son to his father's position as hereditary cup-bearer. This was another way of saying that Ivan's excuse for leaving the service had at least not angered the King. Mazeppa was now free to reconsider his policy and decide what it was best for him to do.

Yet there was a curious aftermath to this period. Passek was still not satisfied and whatever his vices, he had a trenchant and bitter pen and did not spoil a good story. Years later when he came to write his memoirs, he could not resist a last fling at his hated enemy who had risen far higher than he could himself expect.

He told a circumstantial story that Mazeppa was having an affair with the wife of a certain Polish nobleman, Falbowski or Falibowski. Passek was not sure of the man's name, his estate or even the year of the episode. According to him, Mazeppa's suit was so ardent that the husband became suspicious. He very ostentatiously announced that he was going on a journey and then with his servants lay in wait along the road that Mazeppa would have to take to reach his house. The wife at once sent for her lover and Mazeppa soon appeared. It was easy for the husband and his retainers to overpower the solitary horseman. A retainer identified him. The magnate ordered Mazeppa stripped naked, bound hand and foot and tied to his own horse, a spirited animal. The horse was started back at a gallop through the woods, and the nobleman expected that his rival would be killed. He himself went home and used his spurs to good effect on his guilty wife. In the meanwhile Mazeppa was carried back torn and bleeding to his estates and in such a condition that even his servants did not recognize him. Then with his inflated bombast, Passek added: "You see, Mazeppa, what you gain by adultery and rascality? Can one be a liar and a thief, when one is a gentleman?"

This story with its intimation that as a result of this wild ride Mazeppa found himself out of Polish society and so joined the Kozaks at the Sich to which his horse had carried him was too good to lose. Another writer with an even more vivid imagination added that Mazeppa was stripped and then tarred and feathered. His horse dashed into a market place where the weekly fair was being held and dropped dead. The peasants were so sure that Mazeppa was an apparition of the devil that they did not move to release him from the dead horse until they had called the village priest to exorcise this monster who was trying to interfere with their trading by orders of his Satanic majesty.

This is obviously a more embellished form of Passek's story and it is even vaguer for there is no indication of the name of the lady or the injured husband. As for the geographical location there is at least a hint that it happened in a part of Poland that Mazeppa never visited.

Unfortunately or perhaps fortunately when Passek's story reached the Western world, the Romantic movement was in full course. The writers knew little of Mazeppa's history and less of Polish and Ukrainian geography but they recognized a tale which suited their requirements for fantastic adventures and superhuman passions. Both Byron and Victor Hugo and many other authors retold the story in verse in various languages and it is hardly too much to say that today Mazeppa's ride is the chief event connected with his name in the knowledge of the West.

There is a third story that came to light in 1674 in which he was also involved. In that year one Jan Zagorowski, a nobleman of Volyn, brought a suit against his wife Elena Kowalewska. He was apparently an aged grouch married to a young, attractive and flighty woman who did not take her marriage vows too seriously or else the husband wanted to name in her list of lovers any one of prominence. According to one of Elena's ladies-in-waiting, Mazeppa

made her acquaintance, when he was a guest of Dmitri Wisnio-
wecki, the brother of Jarema, the great foe of Khmelnytsky. At
first the lovers met in the gardens but they soon transferred the
scene of their activities to the neighboring woods. To buy the
silence of this lady-in-waiting Mazeppa gave her 10 gold coins
and three strings of beads together with a velvet and sable hat with
coins upon it and he gave four gold coins to another of the suite
and Elena was equally lavish with presents. She added to this the
story that Mazeppa had begged Elena to trick her husband into
going to the village of Reushki where Mazeppa could ambush and
murder the old man. More by luck than by instinct, the husband
after agreeing to go, changed his mind and went elsewhere on
the appointed day. Mazeppa then gave up his pursuit of Elena
and she, losing any hope that her husband could be removed by
violence, invited a relative, one Stanislaw Massalski, to dispose of
the old man by sorcery, while she amused herself with other lovers.
There is something grotesque in this story, for the husband waited
ten years before he decided to bring suit, for apparently Mazeppa
was at the Wisniowiecki's in 1663.

It is hard to treat these stories seriously. Mazeppa like almost
all the gentlemen and ladies of the period was always ready for
pleasure and frivolity. He also had the means to satisfy his whims.
Such affairs and near-affairs were not at all unusual at the time
when the political side of religion all too often dominated the
devotional and the ethical but there is no real evidence that Mazeppa
ever went seriously beyond the general habits of the day.

We can understand Passek's motives because of his desire for
revenge. The other stories may well have been circulated out of
spite and a desire to discredit Mazeppa after he had definitely
broken with Poland or they may have arisen even later after the
battle of Poltava at Russian instigation.

At all events Mazeppa during these years of practical retire-
ment seems to have lived the life of the typical Polish or Ukrainian nobleman with feasting and hunting and entertainment. Yet
we can be sure that he did not neglect the political developments

for it was exactly at this time that the Poles and the Muscovites made peace by dividing Ukraine along the line of the Dnieper and thus once and for all made it impossible for the Hetman, whoever he was, to have sole command of Kozak policy.

Mazeppa was obviously disillusioned by the Polish policy and the unwillingness of the Polish magnates to recognize the services of Ukrainians even when they were loyal to the Polish King. But these years had not been wasted. Mazeppa had become fully acquainted with both the good and bad sides of Polish culture and he had acquired a personal knowledge of Western Europe and especially of French culture. He had become in the fullest sense a Westerner able to think Western thoughts and appreciate Western standards. He had also had a good training in the devious ways of diplomacy both in the West and East and he had learned to keep his own counsel and to remain calm, dignified and unruffled, qualities that were to explain much in his later career.

CHAPTER FIVE

THE SECRETARY OF DOROSHENKO

These years of Mazeppa's withdrawal from public life were tragic years for Ukraine. The Hetman still in theory controlled the entire Host but he was all too well aware that he could not administer it. If the Hetman was inclined to seek for terms with the Poles, he was immediately attacked by the Muscovites who induced the fanatically Orthodox Kozaks, especially the rank and file, to rise against him. If he sought friendship with the Muscovites, the officers were aware of that danger and opposed him, while the ever growing claims of the Muscovites regularly aroused the anger of the Kozaks who were jealous of their own rights and liberties.

In this atmosphere of constant intrigue, the first Hetman to secure some control was Petro Doroshenko. His grandfather had also been a Hetman at a time when the Hetman had few or no political and administrative interests and was primarily the army commander. Doroshenko at the time of his election was Colonel of the Cherkassy Regiment. He was chosen in 1666 and had his seat in the old capital of Khmelnytsky, Chyhyryn, on the west bank of the Dnieper.

His first plan was to deal with the pressing problem of the Poles and to eliminate them from the West Bank and also to recover the province of Galicia with Lviv and the other Western lands. This was of course a popular measure. His first moves were successful and he cleared most of the area along the west bank. It was a pyrrhic victory for it was then that Jan Kazimierz and Tsar Alexis decided on a treaty to divide Ukraine. For a moment even after that it seemed as if Moscow would renounce the treaty in the hope of winning over Doroshenko but it soon became clear to the Muscovites that Doroshenko was also aiming to force their garrisons from the cities on the east bank of the Dnieper and thus menace their own

position. So they decided to respect the treaty. Despite this Doroshenko crossed the river and defeated the pro-Muscovite Bryukhovetsky who had already been forced into revolt and for a while in 1668
Doroshenko was again the Hetman of all Ukraine. Yet when he
was east of the river, the Poles attacked on the west and when he
recrossed, he was faced with new Muscovite intrigues in the east.
He left in command of the east Demyan Mnohohrishny, Colonel of
the Chernyhiv Regiment but it was not long before a new Muscovite
attack, while Doroshenko was busy against the Poles, forced Mnohohrishny to accept again a Russian protectorate and thus more or
less legalize the division of the country as foreseen by the Treaty of
Andrusiv.

This was a hard blow to Doroshenko but he had to accept it
and he did his best to maintain friendly relations with Mnohohrishny and even develop parallel policies. In a real sense this
was impossible.

It was during this period when Doroshenko saw his rule reduced to the west bank that Mazeppa entered his service. There
was perhaps another reason. Mazeppa seems to have had a real
respect for King Jan Kazimierz but the King finally wearied of a
situation where the Polish magnates thwarted his every move and
in 1668 he abdicated and returned to France. The Poles then elected
Michael Wisniowiecki, the son of that Jarema who was so bitterly
anti-Kozak. This made it clear to Mazeppa that peace with Poland
was impossible and so he finally joined Doroshenko.

Mazeppa rose rapidly in his service. His past experiences as
well as his personal abilities soon made him indispensable. Mazeppa
had known Doroshenko previously and had met him on his missions for Jan Kazimierz. He soon became the commander of Doroshenko's headquarters and then the General Secretary and practically
the minister of foreign affairs and for the next years he was im-
mersed in the far flung plans of his chief.

Doroshenko realized that he could not rely upon either Poland
or Moscow and he needed some strong power at his back. There
was only one other choice and that was Turkey which with its vassal

states covered the southern borders of Ukraine. In 1668 Doroshenko placed himself under the formal protection of the Sultan. This of course ran counter to all the Kozak traditions, for they had owed their initial organization to the need for checking Turkish and Tatar raids against the exposed parts of Ukraine. Still there was nothing else to be done. At the same time, whenever possible, he endeavored to strengthen his contacts with all the countries around Poland in the hope that somehow he might be able to free the west bank of the Dnieper.

This gave Mazeppa his opportunity and he was constantly engaged in negotiations with France, for Louis XIV wanted a detachment of Kozaks to serve in the French army. There were any number of questions with the Sultan and the Khan of the Crimea. There were many contacts with the Austrian Emperor, fewer at the time with Sweden for Charles XI had definitely given up his claims to the Polish throne and was pursuing a policy of peace. There were also missions to Samoylovych who had succeeded Mnohohrishny in 1672. In a word Mazeppa's diplomatic missions covered almost all of Central, Eastern and Southern Europe.

He felt himself an important part in the party of Doroshenko and did everything possible to advance both the cause of the Hetman and his own career. He was apparently a coming man on the west bank of the Dnieper.

It was apparently at this time (around 1669-1670) that Mazeppa married. He chose a lady by the name of Anna, the widow of a Colonel Fridrikiewicz and the daughter of Colonel Semen Polovets of the Bila Tserkva Regiment and she brought her second husband a vast fortune, perhaps most of the property of that regiment, for regimental and private property were inextricably mixed. It was apparently a marriage of convenience, for Mazeppa's wife always remained an almost legendary and shadowy figure. She had had one daughter by her first husband and this child died young. She had no children by Mazeppa and though the marriage lasted for some thirty years, we find few or no traces of her influence or even her presence at the elaborate parties of her husband.

For a while Doroshenko's plans for building up Ukraine through the support of Turkey seemed to prosper and the Hetman had high hopes that with Turkish help he might finally destroy the two great enemies of a free Ukraine and once more reunite at least most of the country and shake off any binding and galling obligations.

The situation seemed more promising as time went on. Like most of the Turkish Sultans of the period, Mohammed IV was thoroughly incompetent but there had been placed in power through the harem intrigues a very able Grand Vizier, Ahmed Kuprili. At the very beginning of his service, he had won two great victories over the Christians. He had forced the Venetians to evacuate the island of Crete and by clever diplomacy, he had eliminated the influence of the Holy Roman Emperor in Transylvania and had brought that region as a vassal state definitely under the ægis of the Sultan.

Doroshenko's appeals to him and to the Khan of the Crimea finally aroused in him the dream of adding Ukraine to his laurels. He listened to Doroshenko and then ordered his vassal, the Khan, to aid the Hetman with troops and as a further help, he sent a Turkish force of 6000 men to the Hetman's army.

This was too much for both the Poles and the Muscovites. Both reacted violently and immediately and they hotly threatened all kinds of reprisals against the Turks. Ahmed coldly replied: "God be praised, such is the strength of Islam that the union of Russians and Poles concerns us not at all. Our Empire has increased in might since its origin; nor have all the Christian kings that have leagued against us been able to pluck a hair from our beard."

For the Polish benefit, he added that the Kozaks, a free people, had placed themselves under the Poles but that they were unable to endure the Polish oppression any longer and had now sought the protection of the Turkish Sultan. His power was able to defend them and if the Poles desired war, they could have it and they would be sure that God would give the victory to Islam as He had during the last thousand years.

Ahmed Kuprili wasted no time in words. In the early summer of 1672, a large Turkish army under the command of the Sultan himself invaded Ukraine. It was joined by Doroshenko with 12,000 Kozaks. Its first objective was the Polish fortress of Kamyanets Podilsky which the Poles had manned so as to strengthen their hold on Ukraine. The fortress fell after a slight struggle and the Turks and Ukrainians pressed on toward Lviv. Neither the Polish King nor the magnates, ready as they were to oppress the Ukrainians, had any taste for continuing the war against the victorious Turks. In October of the same year they hurriedly signed in Buchach a treaty of peace and turned over to Turkey the entire Ukraine on the west bank. Turkey directly occupied the province of Podillya and placed Turkish troops in Kamyanets and Doroshenko as a vassal retained the provinces of Kiev and Bratslav. The next year despite the treaty of peace, Jan Sobieski, a competent general, renewed the war more or less on his own and defeated the Turks at Khotyn.

This Turkish triumph in 1672 and the stroke by Sobieski showed the fatal weakness in Doroshenko's plans. He had sought Turkish help as a counterbalance to the intrigues of Poland and Moscow. He had not calculated on Turkish occupation. The Mohammedan rulers and officers were no more merciful than the Christians. They ravaged the country right and left, they seized Christian girls for the harems of the Sultan and the lords, and what was still worse to the Orthodox Kozaks, they showed no respect for the Orthodox Churches. They plundered some, they turned others into mosques, and wantonly desecrated still others.

It was now clear that if war began again, Ukraine would be plundered by three powers and not by two and the third was perhaps the most greedy. The country was completely devastated and the Kozaks and peasants began to flee by the thousands across the Dnieper and into the so-called Land of Free Communes around the present Kharkiv where Muscovite rule was not too firmly organized. The misery and suffering was so intense that even the Chroniclers of the day spoke of the period as the Ruin and when in 1674 a Muscovite army together with the Kozaks of Hetman Samoylovych crossed to the west bank, they were warmly welcomed.

The result was now obvious. All of those people, officers and the rank and file, who had supported Doroshenko and shared his hopes, now turned on him. Where he had been warmly applauded, he was now cursed and execrated. In the reaction against the Turks, part of the Kozaks demanded a new Hetman, Khanenko, who was pro-Polish and part looked longingly toward Samoylovych. Doroshenko's star was beginning to set just as the stars of all the other Hetmans after Khmelnytsky.

At this period Mazeppa, still loyal to Doroshenko, summed up the situation in a duma which was secretly circulated throughout the army among men of all classes. This expressed his own political convictions and it was perhaps one of the few statements of his political beliefs. It shows how far he had moved since his support of the Treaty of Hadyach which was to have included Ukraine as a third and equal member of the Polish Republic.

> Every one for peace is seeking,
>   But on different ropes they're pulling.
> One goes right, another leftward,
>   And it's strange, for they are brothers.
> You've no love, you have no union,
>   Since the day of Zhovte Vody.[1]
> Into anger all have stumbled,
>   For themselves, they've fought and plundered.
> It is time for you, my brothers,
>   To be sure you're not all masters;
> All have not the gift of knowledge,
>   And the wit to govern wisely.
> Take a ship as an example,—
>   You can see the crew is many,
> But one man is known as captain,
>   And he orders all the vessel.
> The poor bee obeys its mistress,
>   In the hive it does her bidding.

---

[1] The scene of the greatest victory over the Poles by Khmelnytsky in 1648.

Lord, have mercy on our Ukraine,
    Where her sons are always fighting.
One, with Infidels agreeing,
    Calls aloud: "Come here, ye Moslems!
Come and save our mother country,
    We will not let her be ruined."
One obeys the Poles for money,
    And laments for his poor Ukraine,
"Oh, my dear and aged mother,
    Why have you become so feeble?
They have cut you into pieces;
    Now the Turk is on the Dnieper.
It is but a scheme to harm you,"
    And a third relies on Moscow,
And he serves sincerely, truly;
    He again still loves his mother.
And he curses her misfortune,
    "Better we had not existed,
Than to live amid this ruin."
    On all sides her foes are fighting,
With the sword and fire ruin,
    Masters are no longer trusted,
Nor respected by their lessers.
    Better 'twere one day to gather.
All to fight against the evil,
    No one by himself can conquer;
He will but prolong the evil,
    Come, ye generals, together.
Why are you so deep in slumber?
    Come, ye colonels, all together.
Give up politics and intrigue,
    Give your hands to one another.
Do not let your mother longer
    Suffer all these frightful torments.
Go, wipe out the hostile armies,
    Load your muskets for the battle,

Sharpen well your keen-edged sabres,
  And if for the Faith you perish,
You are guarding Freedom also.
  Glory be to him eternal,
Who defends his rights with weapons.

This duma sums up Mazeppa's political philosophy and it can explain all of his later actions. It was a noble call for the ending of that civil and military factionalism that had reduced the once mighty Zaporozhian Host to impotence and was ruining the Ukrainian people. Its defects are equally obvious for Mazeppa was an educated gentleman of his day. He was not a scholar, a philosopher, far less a political theorist. It must therefore be interpreted in the terms of his own reading and experience and not in terms of modern thought.

It was a call for the unity of Ukraine and the formation of a true Ukrainian party and government. That had been the dream and the work of Bohdan Khmelnytsky. But what were to be the relations of Ukraine with her neighbors? Where was the standard to be erected? Where was the line to be drawn as to which country was the best ally and what was slavish submission to that ally's interest and not service to Ukraine? The duma offers no guide.

Mazeppa undoubtedly had a good knowledge of the history of the Zaporozhian Host. He knew that in the old days it was the military discipline of the Kozaks that gave them success on their expeditions. He knew their turbulent assemblies at the Sich that made and unmade Hetmans. But in terms of the Host as he knew it, he believed that it was the Officers' Council that should have this power, not the disorderly meetings that had put Bryukhovetsky and similar men into control. The duma thus only expects the individual Kozak to love and obey his officers. Mazeppa's entire training and education had taught him no understanding of the common man. He could not have and in fact did not have any interest in developing that spirit of mass loyalty that Bohdan had fostered.

On the other hand we can well believe that his studies of
Cicero and Plutarch at the Kiev Academy are reflected in it. He
was familiar with the history of the Roman Republic with its consuls and temporary dictators set up by the Roman Senate. He undoubtedly compared the Hetman to the consuls and the Officers'
Council to the Senate and the ordinary Kozaks to the Roman people
whose opinions were less and less respected as time went on. These
were the common ideas of the Academy and Mazeppa could have
no conception of any other form of government except the glorified
anarchy of the Poles and the absolute autocracy of the Tsars.

The duma was certainly a condemnation of the policy of Doroshenko and it undoubtedly spurred the growing discontent throughout all ranks in the organization. Doroshenko was aware of his
growing unpopularity and becoming more and more suspicious of
all around him. Somehow Mazeppa was not suspected of being the
author of the duma and he continued to retain Doroshenko's confidence.

Voices were raised that Mazeppa should become the next
Hetman. He did not encourage them, for he well knew that Doroshenko's successor would be faced with the same factionalism unless
there could be formed a general agreement between all the higher
officers on both banks of the Dnieper and that was impossible so
long as the foreign sovereigns were able to enforce their will on
Ukrainian soil and put garrisons in the Ukrainian cities.

As the situation darkened, Doroshenko became still more dependent on the Sultan and the Khan but he realized also that if his
power fell below a certain point, those powerful figures would
finally turn on him and replace him. Each appeal to the Mohammedan rulers only weakened himself and ruined his people and
alienated more of the persons on whom he had to rely.

Doroshenko became desperate. An abandoned and pathetic
figure, he made a last effort to secure more help by sending to the
Crimea a group of Christian prisoners caught ravaging the Turks,
to be sold into slavery. Doroshenko knew that this was a dangerous
policy and might mean his final ruin. But he had no other way out.

In 1674 for carrying out this plan, he selected Ivan Mazeppa to be the person in charge of the transaction. It was an unpleasant task for that proud Kozak officer who had only recently been pleading for a unified Ukraine. Doroshenko then became fearful that Mazeppa might use this opportunity to desert him and he bound him by a strict oath before the Orthodox Metropolitan of Kiev that he would return.

Fate decreed otherwise.

CHAPTER SIX

THE CAPTURE OF MAZEPPA

Mazeppa tried in every way possible to avoid this unpleasant task of taking Ukrainian prisoners to the Turks but Doroshenko was insistent and even a request to leave the service of the fading Hetman and to join his wife on her estate near Korsun was met with an absolute refusal. Apparently Mazeppa was still the one man who held Doroshenko's confidence. Besides he had been carrying on the negotiations with the Sultan in happier days and Doroshenko could not afford to risk sending a less experienced man on this important mission. He gave his ambassador the warmest letters of introduction and many other important documents.

The little group set out in June. Mazeppa had with him a guard from the Kozaks of Doroshenko and he also travelled with a group of Tatar officials who had been sent from the Khan of the Crimea to Doroshenko. Everything promised a peaceful journey for the group was large and sufficiently varied in composition to establish friendly contacts with any wandering party of Ukrainians or Tatars —with one strong exception. That was a party from the Zaporozhian Sich of those irreconcilable Kozaks to whom any Mohammedan was a sworn enemy. They had been the open foes of Doroshenko in his efforts to secure Mohammedan help and they were not above plundering any detachment that was apparently coming from the Hetman. With Christian prisoners from the Sich in the closed carts, their anger would have been redoubled.

One day as the little band was slowly moving across the sun-parched steppes, the alarm was sounded that a Zaporozhian force had come into sight. What was worse, it was under the direct command of Satan Sirko, the Koshovy or head of the Sich at the moment and well known as a ruthless raider and a daredevil. Sirko, following the tradition of the Sich, maintained his wife and family in the neighborhood of Kharkiv and lived most of the time alone amid the hard-riding and hard-fighting Kozaks who scorned the comforts and the luxury that marked the high Kozak officers.

Sirko for his part noticed first the Tatars and their presence with Kozak officers made him at once suspect that this raid was going to be really profitable. Without a moment's hesitation he and his men launched an attack. They were in overwhelming force and resistance was hopeless. The Tatars, well aware of Sirko's reputation, put up no opposition and scattered in a vain attempt to secure their own safety. Mazeppa's Kozaks were, as always in such cases, inclined to make common cause with the Zaporozhians and Mazeppa, abandoned by all, saw himself exposed to Sirko's vengeance.

That was certain to be worse when the prisoners were discovered. The battle was over in a few moments and the Kozaks rushed in for the booty. It exceeded their expectations. Once they had ripped the covers from the carts, they seized all of the rich gifts that Doroshenko was sending to the Sultan and then they found the prisoners in chains.

Mazeppa's life hung upon a hair. The Kozaks clamored for the death of every one who might be responsible in any way for this violation of the Kozak code. But Sirko recognized the leader of the group and decided to save him. Perhaps he had visions of winning him over to the cause of the Sich which like Doroshenko needed at least a small number of educated men to handle the somewhat limited peaceful contact with Doroshenko, Samoylovych and other leaders. It was impossible for him to control his infuriated band but he succeeded in holding them back long enough for Mazeppa to plead his own case.

There is no record as to what Mazeppa said. A skilled orator and accustomed to the ways and manners of the Zaporozhians, he was finally able to calm them enough so that they resolved not to kill him on the spot but to take him as a prisoner to the Sich. This at least gave Mazeppa a few days to figure out his plan of action.

It was a very bedraggled and crestfallen Mazeppa that finally was deposited among the rude huts of the Sich. The Kozaks gathered around the returning band, eager to learn the results in terms of the booty taken in the raid. Naturally they were overjoyed at the wealth that had been seized but when they learned of the Christians being taken to the Sultan, their wrath flamed up again and they loudly called for Mazeppa's blood. Once again Sirko was able to calm them. He told of the past services and career of the prisoner and he advanced the proposal that Mazeppa would be an asset to the Sich, if his life were spared. His words had some effect for he was well known at the Sich as the most bitter enemy of the Kozak officers of the settled northern regiments, and once again Mazeppa was given a chance to plead his own case.

Again he showed himself equal to the occasion. He used all of his skill and threw the blame upon Doroshenko and explained that he had been compelled to obey the orders of the Hetman. He referred glowingly to the Kozak love of liberty that was burning most brightly at the Sich. He referred to the Kozaks under their favorite title as Zaporozhian Knights and finally when he saw that he was beginning to sway their feelings, he asked to be admitted to the Sich as a refugee. He won his point and the men who had been clamoring for his death now greeted him as a new found brother, for the Zaporozhians did not do things by halves and any one whom they accepted, they received into their own brotherhood.

That night Mazeppa and Sirko could review calmly the whole Kozak situation. They represented the two opposing Kozak camps that had caused so much injury to Ukraine. Sirko was a fighting man with the most rudimentary conception of the problems of administration except as it involved the Zaporozhian supplies of food and equipment. He refused to recognize any Hetman on either bank of the Dnieper and insisted that Hetmans could only be elected as in the past at the Sich and condemned all the pretensions of the Kozak officers. Mazeppa was the opposite. An aristocrat of the aristocrats, a high officer and a wealthy man, a former Polish courtier and a trusted aide of Doroshenko, educated and travelled, he seemed to have come from a different world. Neither convinced the other but both kept their tempers under control and the discussion went on amicably, probably along the lines set out by Mazeppa in his duma.

Mazeppa was at the Sich about five weeks. He realized that it was impossible for him to reenter the service of Doroshenko whose cause had been completely discredited by the attempt to send slaves to the Sultan on whatever grounds. His estates were on the west bank and as they consisted chiefly of land, he could not move them across the Dnieper and he would not go to Samoylovych as a suppliant. He knew that the Sich would protect him and he could wait for some new shift of events.

This was not long in coming. Prince Romodanovsky, the Muscovite commander on the east bank, and Samoylovych soon learned of the great prize that Sirko had captured and they demanded that he be sent to the Hetman's capital at Baturyn. Sirko and the Sich refused as was their custom. This, however, was a special case and when he was thwarted, Samoylovych arrested Sirko's family and threatened to have them sent to Siberia or punished otherwise if the orders of the Muscovites were not obeyed. Faced with this threat, Sirko yielded and in a short time Mazeppa, not a prisoner nor yet released, was on his way.

He had no sooner arrived than he was met by Samoylovych. This Hetman, although under the domination of the Muscovites, ardently desired the union of Ukraine on both banks. Samoylovych however received him coldly and formally and made him feel that he was still in effect a prisoner despite Sirko's promises. He wanted Mazeppa to talk and reveal Doroshenko's plans and aspirations.

Mazeppa's task was now quite different from that which he had had with the Zaporozhians. Samoylovych was himself a Kozak officer with some education and administrative sense. Mazeppa adopted a quite different manner and in a short time Samoylovych began to unbend. Mazeppa talked with apparent frankness about the weaknesses of Doroshenko's position of which he had definite knowledge and when Samoylovych asked him to enter his service, Mazeppa accepted at once. He really had no choice in the matter for Samoylovych could very easily have turned him over to the Muscovites who would have had no scruples about sending him to Siberia or executing him on the spot.

After two days Samoylovych himself began to become uneasy under Muscovite pressure. Mazeppa was too prominent a person, he had been too close to Doroshenko and he knew too much to disappear without a trace as a new recruit in any official rank. His arrival might seem to the suspicious boyars the result of some conspiracy between the two rival Hetmans. So Samoylovych decided to strengthen his own position by sending Mazeppa with Doroshenko's documents on to Moscow with an explanation of his own policy. Of course he assured Mazeppa of his full protection but Mazeppa knew already too well what reliance he could place upon this, if the Muscovites did not choose to recognize it.

There was nothing to be done and Mazeppa started off on the long journey. He cheerfully accepted Samoylovych's advice to be frank and his hope for a quick return to Baturyn.

In Moscow Mazeppa was coldly met at first by many of the clever and intriguing boyars, especially Matveyev who was appointed to examine him as to the plans of Doroshenko. He once again went through the investigation successfully and so impressed the boyars that their mood changed and they too became convinced that they had secured a reliable person to help them against Doroshenko and to carry out their own plans. They encouraged him to accept the offer of Samoylovych and he became very friendly with some as Prince Golitsyn, the leader of the pro-Western party in Moscow. He was invited to their feasts and he did his best to impress himself upon all whom he met.

His visit was successful and when a short time later he returned to Baturyn, it was with a feeling of satisfaction that he had turned an apparent disaster into a personal triumph. He had laid the foundations for a new career in a new part of Ukraine and in his early forties, he was beginning again as the trusted friend of Samoylovych under the Muscovite ægis.

CHAPTER SEVEN

THE AIDE OF SAMOYLOVYCH

On Mazeppa's return to Baturyn, Samoylovych greeted him warmly and was overjoyed that his new friend had won the sympathy and support of the Muscovite authorities. Moscow was a notoriously unhealthy place for prominent Kozaks but Samoylovych had guessed correctly when he thought that Mazeppa's charm and tact would enable him to find his way through the intricacies of Muscovite formalism and intrigue. He now accepted him wholeheartedly and looked for the place to use him.

For his part Mazeppa had a chance to reflect upon what this latest change in his career meant. He had fared better than he had dared to hope when he had been seized by Sirko and his men. Yet he could not overlook the obvious results of his latest decision.

His first task was to bring his wife across the Dnieper. This offered few difficulties and she was the only person for whom he had to be concerned. His sister was married to a Pole and of course living on her husband's estates. His mother was a nun in Kiev and that city was now legally under Russian influence, for in 1670 the time had passed when Poland could have recovered it under the Treaty of Andrusiv. The Ukrainian Orthodox Church was still nominally dependent upon the Patriarch of Constantinople but Russian pressure to transfer it to the Patriarchate of Moscow was growing and Samoylovych made little secret of his desire to see this happen, as soon as a compliant Metropolitan could be elected.

His mother's presence in Kiev was a great source of comfort and help to Mazeppa. She had always had a great influence upon him and he valued her judgment. Besides she was rising rapidly in the religious life and was soon to become abbess of the most important and flourishing convent in Kiev and this brought her into close contact with the leading Kozaks and Muscovites in the city and she could keep him informed on all the newest developments in Moscow where the Patriarch still played an important role.

These were the positive aspects but there were many negative sides as well. All his life he had had the backing of a large and influential family. The Mazeppas were prominent in the region of Bila Tserkva and it was family prestige that had secured him a place at the Polish court and with Doroshenko. Now that influence could not help him. In fact any stressing of his family connections in view of the situation in a divided Ukraine might only create suspicion in the mind of Samoylovych and still more among the Muscovite boyars.

In addition to this Mazeppa realized that he would not be personally welcome in his old haunts. By crossing the Dnieper and making peace with the Muscovites, he would be regarded by his clan as a traitor. It was perhaps not mere chance that it was just at this time that the episode of eleven years before with Elena Zagorowska was raked up with the idea of involving him. The Poles were always ready to belabor a Kozak, especially one who had become openly hostile, and to destroy any influence that he might have kept west of the Dnieper. They publicized all the peccadillos and scandals which they had glossed over, when they were still hoping to use him.

His financial situation was still more serious. He could hope to recover some of his movable assets and he undoubtedly did then or when Samoylovych crossed the Dnieper in 1674 and endeavored with Muscovite support to get control of the region west of the river. But his chief wealth was in land and this could not be moved or disposed of to advantage. He was reduced to actual poverty and although Samoylovych gave him a small estate, he was for a while unable to buy even a pair of bullocks to work it.

Under these circumstances his one recourse was in the service of Samoylovych. In this he was counted as a Military Companion, one of the ranks of Kozak officers directly attached to the Hetman. In the older times (and it was true still in the Sich) service was voluntary and the Kozaks received only their share of the booty taken on the raids. But this system was soon found inconvenient when the fixed regiments were established and their officers assumed administrative functions. The officers needed a permanent corps of assistants for both military and civil functions. The money of the individual officers and the units was inextricably confused and almost imperceptibly the officers became a Kozak nobility and the rank and file drifted toward the position of a peasantry. Every officer of command from the Hetman to the local captain had his own permanent staff. The Hetman as the chief of the state not only had this, the Military Companions, but what was in effect a small but efficient regular army. Of course the men of the Sich considered this a breach of the Kozak tradition and they sneered at the Hetman's forces as mercenaries and hirelings and applied to them any other epithets that they could imagine. Yet it was this situation that gave Mazeppa his chance.

A stranger from across the Dnieper, he had none of those family connections or personal estates which gave relative independence to the colonels and most of the other officers. He had to remain constantly with Samoylovych and be always on duty but he was free also from the temptations to neglect his official duties for personal pleasures.

It also allowed Mazeppa to remain outside the intrigues and the jealousies of the various colonels. As west of the Dnieper, the various colonels were constantly seeking to advance their own position. They too had wealth and prestige behind them and they were often tempted to look down upon and try to thwart the Hetman's plans directly or by intrigues with the Muscovites who had a more pervasive and powerful influence than the Poles had in the west. The King was not as liberal with his gifts nor was he as ruthless in punishing all who fell into disfavor.

It was a humiliating position for a man as proud and haughty as Ivan Mazeppa but he was no longer the young and enthusiastic courtier that he had been when he had denounced Passek to King Jan Kazimierz. Time and experience had made him a cautious and able diplomat with a perfect control of his emotions. Unfailingly courteous and tactful, he maintained good relations with all the different factions, because he impressed upon them that he was merely an agent of the Hetman and had no policy of his own. Self-will and independence were luxuries reserved for those men who had the wealth and the power to enjoy them. They were not for an industrious and devoted servant of the Hetman.

Day by day this apparent selflessness paid Mazeppa good dividends. He became more and more necessary to the Hetman. The colonels and the Officers' Council found him invaluable in bringing their problems before the Hetman. His obvious impartiality was so unlike that of the average self-seeking officer that the popularity of Mazeppa and the confidence of the officers in him grew steadily. He rapidly rose in the hierarchy of Kozak officialdom but always outside the regimental organizations. Finally in 1682 he was appointed the General Osaul or Inspector General and became the openly recognized right hand of Samoylovych.

Almost as soon as he had entered the service of Samoylovych, he was compelled to join his new chief in a campaign across the Dnieper. This was an answer to the disastrous efforts of Doroshenko to strengthen himself and Ukraine with Turkish help. The reaction against this on the west bank ruined Doroshenko completely and after Samoylovych besieged him in his capital at Chyhyryn in 1676, he gave up the struggle and surrendered to Samoylovych and Moscow. He was removed from Ukraine and died in exile in Moscow in 1698.

It is easy to imagine the feelings of Mazeppa as he was thus forced to turn against his old chief. All his life he had tried not to be involved in the interminable civil wars which were only ruining the population but at this moment he had no choice. Yet this defeat of Doroshenko did not help for the Turks put up a new candidate as Hetman, the long forgotten Yuri Khmelnytsky, and despite the efforts of Samoylovych, because of Muscovite delays, they captured Chyhyryn after a long siege in 1678. By now the country was so ruined that the Muscovites lost interest in it and the next year Samoylovych was compelled to evacuate it. He forced a large part of the population to cross the Dnieper and thousands more fled voluntarily to the east into the so-called Land of Free Communes which was technically under loose Muscovite control and not in the area under Samoylovych.

Mazeppa played a role in all these attacks and counter-attacks but his real strength was in diplomacy and it was here that he could give the most help to Samoylovych. From his first visit to Moscow, he had understood the nature of the Muscovite regime and he was fully aware of its aims and purposes toward Ukraine.

He realized that Samoylovych with all of his desires to unify and help Ukraine was but a pawn in the hands of Moscow. The Hetman had married his daughter to the son of Prince Sheremetev, the Muscovite governor of Kiev who was all-powerful in Ukrainian affairs. His sons spent much of their time in Moscow, and the Hetman could do nothing without Muscovite approval. However he was himself torn between his desires to keep them there to support his policy and to bring them back to responsible positions at home. He finally chose the second course and appointed one colonel in Starodub and the other colonel in Chernyhiv.

Mazeppa profited by this. Soon Samoylovych began to send him on important missions to the Russian capital and this allowed him to establish his own contacts there. Year by year with his ever more frequent visits, he made more and more friends among the influential people, the circle around Prince Golitsyn, the lover of the Tsarevna Sofia, the practical regent for the two young Tsars Ivan and Peter.

His devotion to duty as he understood it and his careful avoidance of any of the numerous intrigues among the colonels constantly increased his prestige in all quarters and especially those on which his future depended. Samoylovych, delighted by his fidelity, gave him larger and larger gifts of land and money and at the same time his position in Moscow insured him others from the Russians. By this time Samoylovych was so circumscribed by the Muscovites that he could scarcely make liberal gifts without their permission but this was always forthcoming for Mazeppa who was in their good graces.

For years he did not express his own ideas. At Baturyn, he accepted the Hetman's word as law and he accepted the Muscovite policies as correct but he listened to criticisms of both with the same courteous but non-committal manner. He pursued the same course at Moscow and the Hetman, the officers and the Muscovites regarded him as a coming man.

For the moment he seemed to have forgotten his stormy youth, his aspirations for a free and united Ukraine and all of the ideals for which he had spoken. He seemed the typical courtier and bureaucrat, obeying orders and asking no questions. It pushed him still further along the road to success.

It naturally did not add to his popularity among the Kozak masses who were grumbling at the increasing exactions that were demanded of them by the officers and the Hetman. Samoylovych to maintain himself in power and make larger and larger gifts to Moscow increased the taxes and reduced the few rights and privileges the ordinary Kozaks still possessed. The officers followed his example and each in his own way sought to assimilate his position to that of the Russian boyar or the Polish landlord.

In the meanwhile Moscow planned a new extension of its power at the expense of the Ukrainian Orthodox Church. On the death of the Kievan Metropolitan in 1684, Samoylovych secured the election of Bishop Prince Hedeon Svyatopolk-Chetvertynsky who was in favor of placing the Church under the Patriarch of Moscow. At the election Mazeppa seems to have acted as the representative of the Hetman and argued for the change as the mouthpiece of Samoylovych.

Yet there was one obstacle, if the change was to be made. It had to be approved by the Patriarch of Constantinople who was helpless in the hands of the Turks. They would never allow him to consent while Moscow and Turkey were at war. So peace was in order. In 1681 peace was made between the Tsar and the Sultan. By this the Tsar turned over to the Sultan a large part of Ukraine on the west bank of the Dnieper and provided that the central and southern parts of the province of Kiev should remain uninhabited as a barrier between Moscow and Turkey. Here was a reversal of policy with a vengence. There had been a loud outcry by Samoylovych and all the Kozaks when Doroshenko had carried through this same policy ten years before to form a firm base for uniting the two halves of Ukraine. It had been one of the chief reasons for the fall of that Hetman. Samoylovych had tried to profit by it and now he was compelled to accept a new division of Ukraine despite the promises made to him by the Muscovite authorities.

Naturally Mazeppa was the representative of Samoylovych at the signing of the treaty. He went with the delegations to the Khan's palace at Bakhchisaray in the Crimea and was received there with honor. The bitter irony of the occasion struck him. It was less than ten years before that Doroshenko had sent him on the same mission. That mission had changed his life. It had stripped him of his wealth and position. It had separated him from his old friends. It had subjected him to vilification and scandal. It had nearly cost him his life at the hands of the Zaporozhians. Now he was again commissioned to carry through a division of Ukraine that was even more unfavorable to the people and was being rewarded for it. The lack of unity which he had deplored was producing strange fruits.

Even stranger things were to come. On the west bank of the Dnieper King Jan Sobieski, formerly the bitter foe of Doroshenko and the Kozaks, the man who had destroyed the Kozak organization, was now trying to reorganize the old regiments which he had broken up. He reestablished the Hetmanate under Samiylo Samus and among his colonels was Semen Hurko-Paly, one of the ablest of the western Kozaks. Yet it was not so easy to rebuild what had been hard to destroy and the revived Western regiments never recovered their old prestige.

However they did accompany King Jan Sobieski to the defence of Vienna in 1683 but that victory which saved central Europe brought no improvement to Ukraine. Rather the defeat of the Turks under the new and less competent Vizier Kara-Mustafa strengthened the hold of both Poland and Moscow on the unfortunate Kozaks.

It did facilitate the transfer of the Orthodox Church from Constantinople to Moscow and at once there began a restriction of all those rights of publication and of free activity that the Ukrainian Orthodox bishops had had. Moscow was going to allow no exceptions.

For Mazeppa this was again a personal gain. His mother, the Abbess Mary Magdalen, was now directly under the Patriarch of Moscow and the growing centralization forced her to make many visits to the Russian capital and establish close contacts there for the sake of her convent. It strengthened her grasp upon current events and gave her son still more access to the tangled web of diplomacy.

Mazeppa could not fail to see the significance of all these changes but he was completely helpless. At the very moment when these events were taking place, Samoylovych with the main forces of the Kozaks was completely immobilized, while Moscow was almost openly planning to strip them of still more power. Once again bad timing, so long the curse of Ukraine, was doing its unholy work. Rashness had ruined much. Excessive caution was as dangerous for it only facilitated the betrayal of plans, senseless intrigues and a resulting chaos.

Yet Mazeppa could see something else. The tide was beginning to run against Samoylovych. The Hetman was steadily losing popularity not only among the ordinary Kozaks whom Mazeppa discounted, but also among the officers. Discontent was growing. In the old days as he well knew by experience, there would have been a violent outbreak and the Hetman would have been summarily removed. That was impossible so long as Samoylovych had the favor of Moscow. Yet sooner or later the malcontents would find their way to the ears of the suspicious boyars and Samoylovych, innocent or guilty, would be doomed. Who would succeed him? Perhaps it would be he himself, Ivan Mazeppa, the best known of the Kozak officers in Moscow. Events were taking shape, not without his own assistance, and he might some day under unfavorable conditions have the chance to apply his own theories. In the meanwhile he showed no sign of interest or comprehension and continued to improve still more his relations with Prince Golitsyn and the other important Muscovites.

CHAPTER EIGHT

ELECTION AS HETMAN

Secure in his Muscovite friendships, Samoylovych neglected the growing dissatisfaction of the Officers' Council exactly as he did the murmurings of the ordinary Kozaks. He felt himself the master of Ukraine and he used his powers for his own aggrandizement and the welfare of his friends. He allowed his rights and powers to be whittled away by the Muscovite authorities and he seemed singularly blind to many of the main issues of the day.

Yet Samoylovych was devoted to the ideal of a united Ukraine on both sides of the Dnieper. He was obstinately opposed to Polish control of Ukrainian lands, to any cooperation between Moscow and Poland, and to any system which allowed the domination of the Polish lords. At the same time he kept urging that the Land of Free Communes to the east, now largely filled with Ukrainian refugees from the devastated west bank, should be placed under Ukrainian control but of course the Muscovites paid no attention and in his blindness and confidence in Moscow, the Hetman could not see the real nature of Russian interference.

During all these years Mazeppa was strengthening his relations in the Russian capital. By now he had become wealthy from the gifts of Samoylovych and Golitsyn. He was lavish in his presents to his benefactors, to Golitsyn, to Sofia and to all who were influential. Yet he was not intriguing against his chief. He knew the accusations that were going around and he always carefully presented the Hetman's defence. These defences were not derogatory to his chief. They rather showed his own familiarity with Kozak affairs and Muscovite policy. With his diplomatic tact, he judged it better to emphasize his own importance than the defects of the Hetman. In this he acted quite unlike the colonels who simply showered the Muscovite representatives with denunciations and took no steps to endear themselves to the higher authorities in the Russian capital.

He knew that the hour of Samoylovych was coming but in the mean-time he did nothing to displease the colonels.

His chance came sooner than he expected and in an unusual way.

King Jan Sobieski was violently anti-Turkish. His victory at Vienna had marked the turn in the fortunes of the Sultan. Within a few years the Turks had abandoned the plains of Hungary and the mountains of Transylvania. The King wanted a league of Christian powers to drive them back further and he hoped to recover for Poland that part of Ukraine which had passed under Doroshenko into Turkish hands. He was not thinking of the Ukrainians but of the Poles. So he approached Moscow for an alliance in a war on Turkey. The Moscow boyars, always greedy for land, were inclined to give a favorable ear to the King's plan. They had dreams of cut-ting south to the Sea of Azov exactly as a century earlier the Mus-covite armies moving down the Volga had reached the Caspian Sea.

Samoylovych was furious. He had consciously or unconsciously strengthened the power of Moscow in the Hetman State. He had aided in bringing the Ukrainian Church under the control of Moscow. Now he objected to this new alliance and he sent one of his sons and Mazeppa to oppose it. Again Mazeppa faithfully obeyed orders but all in Moscow understood that he was merely repeating what he was told to say and he gained no ill will. On the other hand the stock of Samoylovych began to fall and some men in Moscow began to believe that the Hetman might have secret relations with the Khan. It was a bad omen. Still nothing was said aloud but Samoylovych was ordered to make ready an expedition.

Prince Golitysn dreamed of winning a victory over the Crimea equal to that won by the King at Vienna. He knew very little about the country to the south and he decided to leave the capital with a great show of splendor and return with rich trophies. He decided to leave Moscow when the weather became pleasant so that he could have a comfortable march.

Again Samoylovych objected. The old campaigner knew the steppes in summer. He knew that while spring came late in Moscow, the blazing summer sun dried up the steppes and made military operations very difficult. He was again overruled.

Prince Golitsyn and the Muscovite court became still more critical of the Hetman. With their sense of correctness and omniscience they could not understand why the usually tractable Samoylovych had suddenly shown a mind of his own. It seemed very suspicious and his opposition to their desires seemed more serious than all the accusations of his enemies, for in his reluctant obedience he had muttered his opinion of the military judgment and knowledge of Golitsyn. That was almost treason.

The expedition started as Golitsyn planned. When Samoylovych was leaving his palace at Baturyn, his horse stumbled. It was taken as an evil omen, because all of the Kozak colonels recognized the mistake of Golitsyn and knew that a scapegoat would have to be found. Yet it was laughed aside and the old Hetman went on.

The armies met as planned and the march began. Golitsyn was right. The weather was pleasant—until the forces reached the steppes. Then the heat became unbearable. There was no water for the horses or the men. There was no shade. The steppe grass was as dry as tinder. The Muscovite soldiers, less accustomed to the southern heat, suffered more severely than the Kozaks and this was another insult for Golitsyn.

Worse than that, no Tatars were seen. Now and then Kozak detachments would report the presence of small groups but the lightly armed and fast moving Tatars kept out of sight of the marching armies and Golitsyn could report no major or minor victories.

Then on July 13, 1687, the tragedy happened. The Kozaks saw on the horizon in the distance faint signs of smoke. It was the beginning of one of those dreaded steppe fires and in a few moments it seemed as if the entire steppe was ablaze. The Tatars had fired the steppe. Nature and not man had confounded the Muscovite commander and his troops had no means of self-preservation.

It was the Kozaks who came to the rescue. They had dealt with that enemy before and while they dreaded it, they knew at least a remedy. They counterfired and by these backfires and other measures, the army was saved but advance was impossible. The troops could not hope to maintain themselves in the burned area. There was now no food, no water, no fodder and there was only one course open to the proud general—an ignominious return to Moscow. That was incredible. It might even jeopardize the regime. It would play into the hands of the Naryshkin faction. It might even compromise his own position with Sofia. It might do anything.

It did, however, increase the grumbling of the officers and men and Golitsyn did not discourage it, for it gave him a new idea. Could he not prove that it was Samoylovych either through his own men or through their connivance with the Tatars that had fired the steppes? The Hetman had told the truth but he had to be proved guilty, if Golitsyn was to save his face and position.

The officers now had the opportunity that they had long been waiting for. They began to let fall in Muscovite hearing their suspicions of Samoylovych. What they did not say openly, they hinted and their hints no longer fell upon deaf ears.

Ivan Mazeppa was as always the chief means of liaison between the two forces. He spent much of his time with Prince Golitsyn but he was well aware of the mood in both camps and of the effect of these stories both on the Kozaks and the Muscovites. The Prince repeatedly asked him his opinion and as always Mazeppa stoutly defended his chief but with his usual custom, he agreed that the Muscovites had better means of learning the truth than he could have. Of course that did not make his defence of the Hetman sound too convincing, although it did restore the self-confidence of Golitsyn.

The retreat continued. Even before the fire some of the officers, sure that there would be some misfortune, had prepared a denunciation of Samoylovych. Now that was given full credence and on July 22, an order arrived from Moscow for the arrest of the Hetman and a thorough investigation of the catastrophe.

Golitsyn seems to have thrown a guard at once around the Hetman's tent. Samoylovych must have suspected already that he would be made the scapegoat, for he knew well the rumors that were drift-

ing around the two camps. Still he gave no sign and the next morning as usual he attended service in the camp chapel. As he was leaving, one of the colonels walked up to him, took him by the shoulder
and uttered the dread words, "The army calls you." This was the
formula that the Zaporozhian Host had used for more than a century to depose a Hetman. It was a summons that could not be dis-
obeyed. At almost the same moment a detachment of Muscovite
soldiers appeared and seized the unfortunate Hetman. There was
no delay. Samoylovych made no resistance, for he knew it was hopeless. His older son likewise yielded without protest. His second son
protested and was killed on the spot "for raising a revolt."

Golitsyn was still not satisfied. He ordered the confiscation of
all of Samoylovych's property and started him and his older son for
Moscow. From there, without delay, they were sent on to Siberia
where the father died wretchedly two years later.

Now came the question of choosing a new Hetman. He gave the
Officers' Council no time to start intrigues or prepare parties. There
was only one possible candidate who had in any degree the confidence of both Golitsyn and the colonels. Golitsyn mentioned other
candidates for the sake of satisfying the Kozak traditions, especially
the General Quartermaster Vasyl Dunin-Borkovsky but he could be
sure of the outcome. The colonels were all jealous of one another.
They were all bitter rivals. Few of them had close friends in high
circles in Moscow. There was only one man who had the necessary broad connections and who was at least acceptable to all parties.
That man was Ivan Mazeppa. He was particularly acceptable to
Golitsyn. The two men had been old friends and Mazeppa shared
those artistic and cultural tastes which Golitsyn and his circle fostered in Moscow.

Golitsyn carried out the traditional ritual. He assembled the
Officers' Council and the Kozak leaders and asked for a successor
to Samoylovych. Unanimously, timidly at first, and then more and
more emphatically there came the one name, Mazeppa. Golitsyn
put the question three times and solemnly proclaimed: "In the

name of the Tsars, I declare Ivan Mazeppa Hetman of Ukraine and
of the Zaporozhian Host."

With equal solemnity Mazeppa begged to be excused. He
pleaded his own unworthiness, as had all previous Hetmans and
Golitsyn insisted that he obey the decisions of the Host. When it
was over, the General Assembly was called together and the new Hetman received the Kozak insignia on July 25, 1687, and then signed
the treaty presented by Golitsyn establishing the relations between
the Zaporozhian Host and the Tsar.

These were in theory the same as those signed by Bohdan
Khmelnytsky in Pereyaslav in 1654 but they were far from being
identical in text. They were reedited with the election of each new
Hetman and each edition increased the powers of the Tsar over
Ukraine. In the edition adopted at this Assembly there were added
clauses that the Tsar should ratify all gifts of land to the officers.
They provided that the Hetman could not be chosen or removed
without the consent of the Tsar, that he could not remove a general
officer without the Tsar's approval, that the estates of the general
officers would be exempt from all taxes and that they should not
be required to pay any sums to the military treasury. There were no
terms concerning the ordinary Kozaks. Then to promote the eternal
brotherhood of the Host and the Muscovites, the members of the
Host were invited to visit Moscow and intermarriage between Muscovites and Ukrainians was to be encouraged.

These phrases together with those guaranteeing the rights and
liberties of Ukraine seemed innocent enough and the officers accepted
them in the belief that they further freed them from the power of
the Hetman. They did not see or want to see that each clause, far
from strengthening the officers against the Hetman left both officers
and Hetman still more at the mercy of the Tsar and gave him the
right to interfere almost at will in all the affairs of the Host. At the
same time, their direct effect would depend upon the relations between the Hetman and Moscow. They made it more necessary than
ever that the Hetman shape his policy with an eye on Moscow
exclusively and if he succeeded in doing this satisfactorily, he would

have the power to put down all discontent and murmurings so long as he could do it without arousing the suspicions of the Moscow boyars.

Once the articles were ratified, the Officers' Council and the General Assembly reentered the chapel and amid solemn pomp and ceremony, Ivan Mazeppa swore that he would protect the Host and Ukraine and be a loyal supporter of the Tsar.

That evening the new Hetman lavishly entertained at dinner Prince Golitsyn and the higher Muscovite and Kozak officers. There were toasts and speeches and merriment. Golitsyn returned the invitations. Costly presents were exchanged and more were promised when the armies returned home. Food and drinks were passed out to the men of the two armies. No one would have believed that this celebration was being held at the end of a completely unsuccessful campaign and that the only man who had predicted its failure was being hustled off to Moscow as a traitor. Samoylovych was entirely overlooked and forgotten.

As Mazeppa took over his new office, he had no illusions. He, as every one else who thought, realized that the election had been a farce. He may not himself have lighted the fuse that had exploded but he had placed himself in a position to profit by the upheaval. Yet no one dared to speak a word of the truth. All knew that Samoylovych had been made the scapegoat for Golitsyn, his obstinacy and his incompetence but no one said so.

During the ceremonies and the feasts, Mazeppa carried out all the traditional rites that were imbedded in the free Kozak tradition but he knew their unsubstantial character. He knew his future would be difficult. He knew the pitfalls in his path. He had seen Hetmans come and go but none had been so unjustly accused as Samoylovych. He was himself no novice. Almost thirty years before he had entered the Polish service in the hope that the King and the Polish magnates would treat Ukraine as a third equal member in the Polish Republic. He had been disappointed. He had served Doroshenko in the hope that with Turkish help Ukraine could become independent and a truly neutral state. The land had become the battleground of conflicting armies. Now he was Hetman and he knew that his rivals and enemies would say that he had bought the post and had sold himself to Moscow body and soul. He knew that this was not the truth.

He regarded himself as the Hetman of Ukraine in the full sense of the word but he determined that he would not repeat the mistakes of his predecessors. He had early learned the dangers of the rash outbreaks of the ordinary Kozaks. Now he had proof that the officers on whom he had to rely could be as easily moved by personal feelings of jealousy and anger. He had seen the helplessness of Samoylovych against these feelings when they were supported by Muscovite influence. That fate would not be his.

He had one weapon as he had phrased it in his duma. He was the captain of the ship. He was the captain of the ship of the Host and officers and men were to do his bidding. They could remove him, if they wished. They could utter the phrase, "The army calls you" and he had no answer but he had signed an agreement that that could not be done without the consent of the Tsar and he could prevent their saying it. He could hold his tongue or use it only to flatter the powerful. He could use his wealth to buy friends but he would do it with the calm certainty that they would not act against him until some one else paid them a higher price and he could see that they did not receive it.

Time and experience had turned him from a young idealist and dreamer into a polished and apparently soulless diplomat, a worshipper of success. Fate had saved him again and again. It would save him to the end. That was his confidence; he would make it his principle and he would assist fate. In the meanwhile he intended to be the Hetman of Ukraine. He was sure that he had its good in his heart and he intended to be a real Hetman,—in the old Roman sense, a dictator.

As soon as the armies reached the borders of Muscovy, they separated. Golitsyn returned to Moscow to receive thanks for his superhuman efforts in saving the forces after the treason of Samoylovych while that unhappy figure went on to his doom.

Mazeppa had to hurry to Baturyn. He had to secure the treasures of his predecessor. He had to set up his new regime and to do it under adverse circumstances for on August 3, scarcely two weeks after his election, a wave of revolts swept over the country.

They were caused by the ordinary Kozaks who realized all too well that the new articles had given them nothing and the officers everything. Their reaction was to kill the officers and colonel after the colonel was attacked. The Sich as always struck out against a newly elected Hetman from the officer class. No one wanted to see that all these movements weakened Ukraine and strengthened the hands of the Tsar, that they made the presence of Muscovite troops in Ukraine necessary, that they prevented any steps at social reform. Within a year by rigorous methods Mazeppa quieted this movement.

He had to oppose the officers, especially those from the neighborhood of Poltava who refused to understand that they could not bring back the old chaotic times when the colonels made and unmade Hetmans at will.

Then he had to go to Moscow to pay his respects to the rulers and along with him went the Abbess Mary Magdalen on business for her convent. His visit was brief but she remained almost a year in Moscow, learning for herself and her son the intricacies of Muscovite politics. On this occasion he brought rich gifts amounting to over 11,000 rubles for Golitsyn out of gratitude for his many acts of kindness.

Even while he was busy with securing the power, Mazeppa decided that he was going to change the old order and stop the constant inroads of the Tatars. He planned the building of forts along the river Samara in the southeast with Muscovite garrisons to stop these raids. It made no difference that in doing so he could effectively hold in check the Zaporozhians who distrusted him and might turn them in whole or in part toward agriculture, if the profitable raids for booty were checked. He was building for the future. He would cement his own power and then the security of Ukraine. It was a cynical but perhaps a wise choice.

In 1688 there came another campaign against Perekop. Once more he and Golitsyn joined forces and once more he like Samoylovych tried to hasten Golitsyn's start but in his quiet way, Mazeppa got his friend to Perekop before the extreme hot weather and lack of water became fatal. The Tatars opened negotiations for surrender. Once again the Muscovite commander turned to Mazeppa for advice and again with the same courtesy the Hetman refused a definite answer in view of the Prince's greater experience. He approved all of Golitsyn's suggestions and when Golitsyn left before the negotiations were concluded, he left with him. But he did not return to Moscow. Golitsyn pictured this campaign as a triumph. He gave himself far more credit than he deserved and the only person in Moscow who dared to question his glowing reports of triumph was the young Tsar Peter who refused to take part in the triumphal ceremonies.

By that time Mazeppa was safely back in Baturyn. He would not risk casting a shadow on the victory of the Prince. Golitsyn could receive from Sofia all the adulation and presents and they were showered in abundance. Then when the first flush of enthusiasm was past, Mazeppa with his staff arrived in 1689 for a formal visit.

There he was when the Muscovite explosion came and Peter triumphed. The power of Sofia crashed. Golitsyn stole away from Moscow. His estates were confiscated and he moved to the frozen north as a prisoner as ignominiously as he had sent off Samoylovych two years before. He became the scapegoat for Peter while Mazeppa by luck or skill made his peace with Peter and returned to Baturyn, still Hetman of Ukraine and in close accord with the new regime in Moscow.

CHAPTER NINE

THE YEARS OF CALM

The first twelve years of Mazeppa's Hetmanate passed in relative calm. After the first disorders that attended his succession to the post, there were no serious threats to his regime, although there was a sullen opposition among part of the officers and a continuous murmuring of the peasants at the restrictions under which they were compelled to live. Life seemed fairly peaceable, as Mazeppa's new fortresses in the south gradually checked the Tatar raids. To the casual observer it might seem as if nothing had really changed and that Mazeppa was only in a somewhat more gracious way continuing the policy of Samoylovych and placing the interests of Moscow above those of his native land.

In one sense there was some truth in it; yet in another sense it would be a gross misstatement. The political situation had greatly changed. For a few years it seemed as if Moscow were little interested and Poland less so. There was a reason for this. After the death of King Jan Sobieski, the condition of Poland changed for the worse. There was a French and an Imperial party and when finally Augustus II of Saxony was chosen, he used Poland only as a source of income for his court in Dresden and he neither knew nor cared about his realm. There might be a flood of denunciations of Mazeppa emanating from Polish sources and from discontented officers but Peter was on too good terms with Mazeppa to take these seriously.

The situation was the same with Turkey. The defeat at Vienna and the victories of Prince Eugene of Savoy in the south along the Danube left the Sultans small opportunity for interfering in Ukrainian affairs. This in its turn discouraged the efforts of the Khan of the Crimea who adopted a far less aggressive policy.

The Hetman was chiefly concerned with Moscow and after the palace revolution of 1689, the young Peter, now the dominant force in the state, was quite content to allow the Ukrainian situation to develop as it would. He was busy forging his own new system. For the moment he allowed his relatives, the Naryshkins, to run the central government, while he organized a modern army and built a navy. These were enormous tasks and no one either in Moscow, Baturyn or Europe could dream of the use that the young giant would make of them, once they were in a condition that satisfied him. Then in 1697 he went abroad and stayed for two years while it seemed as if Moscow and the streltsy would undo most of his work.

It was against this background that Mazeppa had the opportunity to carry out some of his own ideas and to show his own conception of the true position of a Hetman. It also became evident that the changes made in the Articles which he had signed on his accession greatly increased his own power over the officers of the Host. Slowly but surely he came to dominate the Officers' Council and eliminate most of those officers who were still loyal to Samoylovych or partisans of a free and easy system and he replaced them with his own men whom he could trust. He gave these new appointees extensive estates and liberal gifts. He did this without difficulty, thanks to his excellent relations with Moscow and the confidence that Peter had in him.

He profited by his own experience. He gladly welcomed Kozak officers from the west bank of the Dnieper. Many he had known intimately during his service with Doroshenko. After the fall of that Hetman, they had straggled across the Dnieper and now they were at his disposal for the formation of a permanent administrative corps. Like himself, they had in the beginning no share in the intrigues of the old regimental staffs. Some like Pylyp Orlyk may not have been of Ukrainian origin but they had thrown themselves into the cause of the Zaporozhian Host and Mazeppa welcomed their services.

Mazeppa's chief object was to develop an organized Hetman State which was to take the form of the average Western European state of the day, perhaps a miniature court of Versailles under Louis XIV or an imitation of the Swedish crown. He did not want to

imitate the clumsy and intriguing autocracy of Moscow or the
anarchy of Poland in which the King could not control the magnates and was obliged to sit idly by while the fabric of the government went to pieces. Yet his steps in any direction had to be taken
cautiously, because he was dependent for his success upon the good
will of Peter and of Moscow and he could not move too rapidly
from the beaten track.

This was one of the reasons why he was criticized so frequently
by the masses of the population. He was not able to lighten rapidly
the burdens imposed upon them. He needed the income from the
heavy taxes for his liberal presents to his assistants and the Muscovite
leaders. At the moment when the Russian masses were being subjected to heavier and heavier taxes, too strong an opposite course in
Ukraine would have aroused suspicion.

On the other hand his Universals showed that to some extent
he appreciated the situation. In 1689, before he left Moscow, he
secured from Peter an order forbidding peasants to become Kozaks
and in 1691 he issued an order to all the officials and officers
not to overburden the population with compulsory work. He set the
limits at two days a week and he also forebade forcing the Kozaks
into a position where they would seek to become peasants. His
measures may seem to-day too moderate but he was trying to stabilize
conditions rather than definitely reform them and in the Ukraine
of his day that was the most crying need.

At the same time, he endeavored to develop the industrial capacity
of the country. He established many factories, especially for making
potash, glass, ceramics and weaving, all fields that had been largely
untouched before but which could in time develop beneficial activity.
After the disorders of the preceding half century much of Ukraine
had to be rebuilt from the bottom and that is what he was trying
to do.

Curiously enough there was one field which he neglected, the
building of a modern army, the very centre of Peter's efforts. The
Kozaks had won their reputation chiefly in fighting the highly mobile
Tatars. They were excellent horsemen, highly individualized and

opposed to rigid discipline. They resented that perpetual drilling, that training in rigid formations, that concentration of fire power that marked the continental armies. The Kozak regiments remained, as they had been in the past, intended for the open warfare of the pathless steppes. There, European infantry was obviously useless, for the conditions were different from those in Western Europe where space was at a premium and a line in close formation could decide a battle. So Mazeppa tried to improve the morale of his troops without introducing any fundamental changes in tactics. Yet in doing this, he did not realize that he was moving against the spirit of the times and was in a way reducing the value of the Kozaks for opposing the new Muscovite forces, if it ever became necessary. This lack of trained infantry was later to cost Ukraine dearly, although at the time it seemed that Mazeppa's policy was correct.

There was something incongruous in the relations of Peter and Mazeppa. The one was in his twenties, the other approaching sixty with an eventful and stormy life behind him. The one was practically self-taught, impetuous and energetic with a diabolical drive that knew no limits either in work or in dissipation. Highstrung and irascible, Peter was the very symbol of a revolutionary explosion. Mazeppa, the best educated man at his court, was calm and master of his own feelings. With a consciousness of his own traditions and position, he moved through life like a prince of the Renaissance and not an unconsidered word fell from his lips even in the middle of the wildest, gayest and most unrestrained party, but he was not a spectre at a feast, not a gloomy and suspicious figure but a gracious and kindly host and guest and a model of hospitality and frankness. It is small wonder that European travellers who visited Baturyn regarded him as one of the most highly cultured men in Eastern Europe.

Peter appreciated the Hetman and at this period the feeling was certainly returned despite the fundamental difference in the point of view of the two men. No one else in Moscow held the same anomalous position. To Peter, Mazeppa was a Muscovite officer with some strange independent powers that he could not understand and that somehow offended him. To Peter he was a Russian with some unusual rights which should not be opposed to the Tsar's will. His business went through the routine hands of the men charged with foreign affairs. He was in and out of the Russian realm and was thus distinct from the semi-vassal princes as those of Georgia, who were likewise dependent upon Moscow, because he was a real member of the Tsar's court.

Mazeppa considered himself the Hetman of Ukraine and for all intents and purposes an independent sovereign, the head of a free people but yet acknowledging for practical purposes a certain dependence upon the Tsar who was to support him against all enemies, internal and external, but was not to break the duly signed and authorized treaties. He knew that under the agreements which he had signed, he was not to enter into any formal negotiations with foreign powers but his long experience had provided him with many friends abroad and these gave him a permanent contact with all of the diplomatic circles of Europe and he was thus often able to supplement and correct the reports that were made to Peter himself but he always did it in the most respectful and tactful way without questioning the superior knowledge of the Muscovites.

In this peculiar position and in the same manner he was able to place in high positions in Moscow and the service of its Patriarch many of the most distinguished graduates of the Kiev Academy. During this decade such men as Stefan Yavorsky, later the last *locum tenens* for the Patriarchal Throne, and Dmitri Tuptalenko, later Bishop of Rostov, were brought into the Muscovite service. They had been introduced by Mazeppa to the highest state dignitaries and even to Peter himself and sooner or later they came to fill all the posts that required educated and cultured men. In this way Mazeppa unconsciously drained off the educational élite of Ukraine but it gave a Ukrainian coloring to Muscovite intellectual life and the Tsar, with his fantastic desire to Westernize his country, was deeply grateful for this assistance.

Yet it must be emphasized that it was not a desire for culture that bound the two men together. Peter was vulgar and irreligious. He found his closest cronies in men of the lower classes like Alyosha Menshikov and the hard-drinking and carousing Germans and French whom he had attracted to his court. Mazeppa admired culture, pomp and dignity. Perhaps to some degree Peter envied him this ability but he did not try to imitate him or to pitch the tempo of Muscovite court life on the gaiety and formal splendor that was the constant atmosphere of Baturyn.

Perhaps the two men found more in common in their domestic affairs. Peter was hopelessly bored and disgusted with his wife Eudoxia who shared none of his aspirations for his country. He felt that her influence upon their son Alexis was wholly bad, and that Alexis was being reared as the opponent of all for which his father stood and he was waiting for an opportunity to free himself of her for good and all. Mazeppa's wife was a shadowy figure at best. She was fully in the background. They had no children and the Hetman with all of his strong family feeling was a lonesome man.

He tried to make up for it by his kindness and help for his sister Oleksandra. She was consistently unlucky in her married life. Her first husband Obidowski died soon after the birth of their son Ivan. Mazeppa took the boy and brought him up. He sent him to the Kiev Academy, initiated him into the life of the Kozak Host and he had visions of having him as a confidant.

Oleksandra did not remain a widow long. She soon married another Pole Witoslawski and had a daughter Marina. Again her husband died and the young girl finally came under the influence of her grandmother, the Abbess Mary Magdalen. Finally she too became a nun and disappears from history.

Oleksandra's third husband was again a Pole, Jan Wojnarowski. He was a widower with two daughters at the time of their marriage and once again the marriage was rewarded with a boy, Andrzej-Stanislaw. This marriage was not happy. Like the other members of her family Oleksandra was stoutly Orthodox despite her habit of marrying Catholic Poles. The religious differences flared up and Olek-

sandra appealed to her brother. He arranged for her to come to
Baturyn and although she was again reconciled to her husband, the
old sore remained until her death about 1692. Apparently Wojnarowski did not long survive her for their son and Wojnarowski's
two daughters also came to live under the ægis of the Hetman.

Both Ivan Obidovsky and Andri-Stanislav Voynarovsky (to
give them their Ukrainian spelling), played an important role in
the later life of Mazeppa. It was in their interests that he worked
and he constantly had their good in mind.

Naturally this policy of Mazeppa and his strengthening of his
authority seemed contrary to the democratic traditions of the Ukrainians and especially the Kozaks of the Zaporozhian Sich. The
officers of this still in theory at least and largely in practice
maintained that no Hetman could be elected except at a general
assembly of the Sich and they continued to be a sore spot in the
side of Mazeppa and of the Ukrainian organization which he was
trying to strengthen.

Yet events were compelling the Sich to lose its importance. The
burdened peasants looked to the koshovy of the Sich for protection. They saw in the Sich that freedom which they could not obtain
from the growing control of the Hetman and the colonels. They
still glorified the Sich with its lack of restraints, its wild and turbulent gaiety. The Sich still appealed to the homeless and the dis-
inherited. It still offered the right of asylum to the fugitive and the
outcast. But that was all.

The Kozaks of the Sich still indulged in raids against the Moslems
but they no longer took the rich spoils that they had in the early
part of the century. No longer did their detachments plunder the
suburbs of Constantinople and the harbor of Trebisond in Asia Minor
and rescue the enslaved Christians from the slave-markets of Azov
and Kaffa. The Sich was rapidly becoming a mere refuge for adventurers and ne'er-do-wells from all over Ukraine and it had almost
lost its power to influence events for good or ill. It was now a
nuisance rather than a force to be reckoned with, a headache and
not a problem.

Another reason for its impotence, in addition to the presence of Mazeppa's new forts, was the conception which the Kozaks of the Sich had of themselves. Much as they disliked the power of the officers, they could not long make common cause with the masses of the people. They could receive refugees and fugitives and absorb them into their own ranks, but when the Zaporozhians came into contact with the ordinary peasants, they took great pains to impress upon them that they were the gallant Knights of the Zaporozhian Sich, the equals of the officers, not the democratic brothers of the peasants. It had been apparent for more than a half century that the men of the Sich were far more interested in exalting their own position than in standing for a broadening of the democratic elements in Ukraine. They stormed against Mazeppa and dared to tell him what they thought of him and the officers but they now refused to commit themselves to any rash adventure that might jeopardize the position and liberties of the Sich. In fact they themselves were slowly undergoing that same transformation which had occurred more rapidly when the regular local regiments were established and the officers began to form under Khmelnytsky a new Ukrainian administration to control the more settled part of the country.

They could not and would not make common cause with any remaining opposition among the officers. Nothing shows this better than the case of Petryk which a few years earlier would have led to serious dissensions and perhaps endangered the position of the Hetman.

In 1691 Petro Ivanenko (Petryk), a senior clerk in the General Chancellery of the Army, was sent to carry presents from the Tsar to Colonel Zhuchenko of the Poltava Regiment. He delivered the presents but instead of returning to Baturyn, he went off to the Sich and ultimately became its Secretary. He was not satisfied with its relatively minor role and began to conduct a vigorous campaign to restore it to its old importance. But he had to have support. Where could he find it? He appealed to the oppressed masses but he well knew that they were no match for the armed forces of the Hetman and his Muscovite allies. He could not turn to Poland for there he

would become entangled with the Kozak revival that was being
fostered by Sobieski and would be confronted with the same problems that he was trying to avoid.

So he fled to the Turkish fortress of Gazi-Kerman and there made
an agreement with Kemen-Murza. This was in the form of a treaty
between the Khan of the Crimea and the "Separate Principality of
Kiev, Chernyhiv and the entire Zaporozhian Urban Army and the
Little Russian People" to protect Ukraine from Russia and Poland
and "not to attack our country."

Petryk appealed for a popular uprising against the Hetman and
his professional regiments. It was the type of appeal that had
embarrassed even Khmelnytsky some fifty years before. At that time
the call set the country aflame. The peasants rose and burned the
manor houses of the Polish landlords everywhere. Now the movement missed fire. There were some uprisings, enough to disturb
the Hetman briefly but nothing more. The Muscovite garrisons in
the cities were ready to support the Kozak regiments and even the Sich
itself refused to move wholeheartedly.

This was in a way natural. The wiser heads remembered that the
original task of the Sich had been to fight the Mohammedans. They
remembered the legends of Bayda Vishnovetsky and the other known
and unknown heroes who had suffered at the hands of the Turks
and Tatars. They remembered the disastrous outcome of most of the
alliances with the Crimean Tatars and the damage that had been
done to the Kozak lands by the plans of Doroshenko and they refused to stir.

They applauded the high-sounding proclamations of Petryk and
it is not impossible that Mazeppa himself was not opposed to their
publication, for they were almost what he was himself to say some
years later. Yet there was no effect. Petryk in announcing himself
as the new Hetman, declared:

"It is sad to see how strangers are injuring and ruining our
country. It is not surprising that the King of Poland acts this way.
We were once his subjects but thanks to the Lord and Khmelnytsky,
we have done so much harm to the Poles that they cannot even yet

recover. It is not surprising that the Khan of the Crimea has been our enemy, for since the most remote days we have been ravaging his territory.

"But what is surprising is the conduct of the Tsars of Moscow; they have never conquered us by arms; our ancestors, to serve the cause of Orthodoxy, voluntarily submitted freely to them. Moscow has made of us its rampart; from wherever he comes, the enemy always ravages first our country in the shelter of which Moscow remains as behind a fortress. But that is not enough for the Tsar; he wishes to make us his slaves."

Petryk, who was by no means an ignorant man, delivered these true statements from Akhmachet in the Crimea. He knew Kozak history and he hoped that a declaration of the truth of the last half century would create enough commotion to break the power of both the Tsars and the Hetman officers.

Mazeppa equally well recognized the situation but he knew that the appeals of Petryk for a return to the past would only re-institute that confused anarchy that had proved the ruin of the fabric started by Khmelnytsky, complete the ruin of Ukraine and leave it completely defenceless. He knew that an unrestrained jacquerie with the burning of all the manor houses and the murder of all the educated and cultured leaders of the people was the worst way to found an independent state which could play its part on the European scene and give his people their rightful place. Accordingly he answered Petryk in that aristocratic way that was most natural to him.

"Do we not know that your father was a beggar, that he lived at Poltava on public charity, and that you yourself, when you went to school, wandered in the streets with the beggars and lived on the scraps that we threw out of the windows?[1] You never came near to being a knight. We do not believe that the Khan is with you.

---

[1] This may well be a suggestion that Petryk had been one of those wandering dyaks (scholars who earned their living outside of the Academy by traveling around the countryside, singing and acting—a typical phenomenon of the Ukraine of the day).

We cannot admit that a person of such importance would follow you, a liar, a miserable dog. Probably your Khan is some gypsy who has succeeded among the Tatars in getting together a hundred beggars and now calls himself the Khan."

These are the words of a genuine aristocrat of the day. They are the words of a captain ordering obedience and expressing his surprise at disobedience and revolt. The Hetman brushed aside those parts of Petryk's proclamations that he had himself expressed in his duma of a few years before and that echoed his own thoughts. He was to repeat them later but he was not yet ready and perhaps he hoped that Peter would become a Westernized sovereign and honestly accept Ukraine as a permanent independent state in alliance with Moscow. For the moment he forgot his distrust of Moscow in his hatred for the point of view of Petryk and in his desire to strengthen the position of the officers and to weld together into a real organization the Kozak Host.

This was in 1693. The efforts of Petryk to rouse the people against the Hetman and the Tsar met with failure. Petryk was repudiated by the masses of the Zaporozhians and he retired for the winter into the Crimea under the protection of the Khan. In the spring he again sallied forth. He again issued the same type of proclamations. He again attracted some of the more restless spirits among the Zaporozhians. He roused a small part of the population. There were some more minor operations against him. Petryk disappeared but in 1695 and 1696 he reappeared with the same tactics.

Petryk did accomplish something but not what he had expected. In 1695 Peter decided to take action against the Khan of the Crimea and, if necessary, against the Turkish Sultan. His companion and friend Lefort, who had aided him in his efforts to build a navy, encouraged him to attack Azov at the mouth of the River Don and put himself in a position to profit more thoroughly by the command of the southern steppes and the Volga River but there can be little doubt that this enterprise was warmly approved by Mazeppa. Peter realized that control of the city of Azov at the mouth of the Don would put him in a position for a final attack on the Crimea whenever he wished.

For this campaign Peter under the guise of a captain of the Muscovite navy sailed down the Volga by boat to Tsarytsyn (the present Stalingrad) and then marched the short distance between the Volga and the Don toward his objective. Mazeppa and his Kozaks marched overland and the two armies met near Azov. They assaulted the city from July 8 to September 22. The Kozaks had crossed the steppes before the heat of the summer and so they escaped the fate that had once ruined Golitsyn.

The fortunes of the campaign were little better. Peter had not yet welded the various foreign and Russian detachments, his new troops and the old streltsy, into a coherent whole. Everything went wrong. The mines which were built by one section of the forces blew up another part of their own men. There was general chaos in the ranks and the only victories won were by Mazeppa and his Kozaks who were in their element in fighting the Turks and Tatars. They sustained their reputation for bravery and courage.

Yet the Tsar could not be defeated and on his return to Moscow Peter like Golitsyn before him boasted of his victories and celebrated a triumphant entrance into his capital. Just as before Mazeppa did not wish to detract from the joy of the triumph and he quietly returned to Baturyn with his own forces and merely sent messages of congratulation.

There was however one difference between Peter and Golitsyn. The former was willing to learn. He took the advice of his old friend and tutor, General Patrick Gordon, a Scotsman, and prepared a different strategy for the campaign of 1696. He determined this time to sail down to Azov with his fleet which he had rebuilt on the upper Don near Voronezh and thus was able to assault Azov both by land and sea. Again Mazeppa led his troops overland.

However, by this time Mazeppa was aware of the futility of the threats of Petryk and he set a price on his head. It is still not certain whether this reward was ever claimed. There are tales that he was murdered by a Kozak named Vechorka but there is also evidence that he retired to the Crimea and many years later cooperated with the followers of Mazeppa after the battle of Poltava.

This time the joint expedition was successful. The final assaults by land and sea captured the city and gave Peter the complete control of the Sea of Azov and with it the definite supremacy over the Khan of the Crimea who was henceforth unable to secure help from any of the hordes east of the Don and gradually sank into a position of insignificance without any importance on the international scene. Peter had now won a real triumph.

It was also a definite blow to Ukraine for it put the Muscovites in control of the line of the Don and from henceforth this would form the eastern boundary of Ukraine. The Ukrainians could no longer hope to continue their eastward colonization and extend the domains of the Hetman even into the Land of Free Communes, the land in the neighborhood of Kharkiv where there was a mixed population. The Hetmans had long been trying to secure control of this. There had been some irregular clashes between the Ukrainian and Muscovite settlers but with the new advances of Peter, the question was completely answered and Mazeppa had enough sense not even to raise it.

In March 1697 Peter started out on his celebrated journey to the West. It was the first time in history that a Muscovite Tsar had travelled to Europe, although in the past many, including St. Alexander Nevsky, had journeyed eastward to the capital of the Grand Khan and had lost their lives in the process.

While he was gone, Mazeppa enjoyed a free hand in the organization of the Hetman State. Peter had not the slightest doubt of his loyalty and for his part Mazeppa certainly hoped that personal contact with the West would show Peter the better sides of Western civilization and that this would result in a further and proper Westernization of Moscow. He hoped that it would aid in breaking down that past desire for isolation that had made the Muscovite autocracy and boyars so unwilling to accept anything that savored of Western and even Kievan thought. He was sure that an enlightened Peter would sympathize even more wholeheartedly with his own ambitions for Ukraine.

While Peter was in Europe, Mazeppa was in peace. Peter's representatives in Moscow were hardly in a position to know more about the Tsar's movements than was Mazeppa through his various confidential agents. It was a golden opportunity and Mazeppa in Baturyn made good use of his time.

When Peter returned in 1698 after the revolt of the streltsy in Moscow, Mazeppa of course hoped that Ukraine would immediately profit. In a report to the Tsar, he stated: "During the last twelve years since the beginning of my Hetmanate, I have made 11 summer and 12 winter campaigns and it is not hard for any one to appreciate the difficulties, losses and ruin from these unceasing raids which the Zaporozhian Army and all Ukraine have suffered."

The Tsar was duly grateful. He had executed the leaders of the streltsy and the Muscovite conservatives with his own hand for their part in the revolt and he felt a certain confidence in his friend Mazeppa who had kept that always turbulent Ukraine peaceful but that was all. He had brought back with him to Moscow not the finer sides of Western culture but an appreciation of its material superiority and he was determined as the autocratic Tsar to force his land to an accelerated rate of progress, no matter what it cost.

He had imbibed one touch of true Western formalism. He immediately established the Order of St. Andrew. It was to rival in dignity and grandeur the Order of the Golden Fleece of the Holy Roman Empire and the other orders which graced the courts which he had visited. He was to go them one better and establish an Order in honor of St. Andrew, that Apostle of Christ who by ancient tradition had first preached the Orthodox Faith on the site of Kiev. It was a sign also that Christianity was far older than the Kiev state (the ancestor of Moscow, as he conceived it) and far older than the mission of Saints Cyril and Methodius, the Apostles to the Slavs. It was another example of the greatness of his realm. It was indeed a grandiose conception worthy of the past pride of the Muscovite Tsars. He named as the first member his dearest friend and closest collaborator, Alyosha Menshikov. The second was Ivan Mazeppa, the Hetman of Ukraine and the Zaporozhian Host. It was a sign of the position and prestige of Mazeppa at the imperial court.

CHAPTER TEN

THE PATRON OF CULTURE

This political and economic reorganization of Ukraine did not exhaust the energies of Ivan Mazeppa. He not only remodelled the entire structure of his country politically, he not only defended it in the field, guarded the frontier, kept the Zaporozhian Sich in order and cooperated with the Muscovites in putting down once and for all the menace from the Khan of the Crimea. In addition to all this he maintained the most varied political connections and superintended the internal administration of the country and the maintenance of order.

At the same time he provided for the cultural life of his people. There had been few periods of peace since the establishment of the Hetman State under Bohdan Khmelnytsky in 1648. The foreign invasions and the wars between rival Hetmans had ruined many of the cities. The churches and other public buildings had been plundered again and again. The educational system had been shattered. In addition to this the Orthodox world outside of Ukraine and Moscow was suffering under the anti-Christian policy of the Turkish Sultans and the prestige of the Patriarch of Constantinople and the other Eastern Patriarchs had sunk to a new low. The Orthodox Church as a whole presented a sad picture of ruin and of desolation while the great powers of the day seemingly cared little about the havoc that their policy was causing.

Mazeppa set himself to correct this. He was a hero on the field of battle but he was an educated man trained in the best that Ukraine and the West had to offer and he rose to his responsibilities. Whatever we may think of the narrowness and artificiality of his early education, we have to admit that it remained with him and fired him to introduce a new golden age in Ukrainian and Eastern European culture. For the accomplishment of this he used all the time that was not required for the political and military functioning of his various posts.

It was this emphasis on art, beauty and the humanities that set Mazeppa sharply apart from Peter. The latter, with his superhuman energy, pressed on the task of turning Moscow into a powerful state and emphasized practical accomplishments. It was only in the last years of his life after his foundation of St. Petersburg that he seriously gave his attention to cultural interests and then it was only to produce a city that would outshine the Western capitals externally. It was still later when he turned his thoughts to the foundation of new educational institutions. Before that he had bothered only to send selected students to Western Europe to study such subjects as mining and engineering, navigation and shipbuilding. He ordered the translation only of those books which had immediate practical value either in politics or engineering. He neglected all those aspects of life that we now know as the humanities.

Mazeppa was different. From the very beginning of his regime, he tried to revive the glories of ancient Kiev and Rus and to provide a proper setting for himself and his associates.

Thus the relatively simple buildings at Baturyn which had satisfied Samoylovych did not seem to him worthy of a powerful Hetman. He built a new and more elaborate palace worthy of his rank. Here he housed all the important mementoes of his predecessors. He provided elaborate banqueting halls, armories, a library, all the rooms needed by a cultured and wealthy European gentleman. Here he lived and entertained like a sovereign ruler as indeed he considered himself. Baturyn became a mecca for foreign travellers and the Hetman was praised by all of them as the most cultured man in Eastern Europe.

He did not confine his efforts to the glorification of the surroundings of the Hetman. He was interested in repairing and restoring all the important churches and other ancient buildings in his domains and in building new ones and almost every year saw the completion of some church, some monument, some foundation of the first class.

It was not the age for archaeological restoration. The prevailing traditions of art called for the remodelling of old buildings in the then modern style. That was the Baroque architecture which had come from Italy to France and then especially under the influence of the Jesuits had replaced the older styles of architecture in Poland and the Holy Roman Empire. Mazeppa saw to it that this late flowering of the Renaissance should take root in Ukraine and under his direction carefully selected foreign and native artists created that style which is still known as the Mazeppa or Ukrainian Baroque.

Take for example the ancient Cathedral of St. Sofia in Kiev. It had been built by Yaroslav the Wise in 1037. It was in a sad state of ruin. The Metropolitan Petro Mohyla in the early part of the seventeenth century had worked upon it and made it relatively strong and durable. Now Mazeppa almost completely remodelled it. He added towers and domes, he made windows in the walls and adorned them with the Baroque ornaments of the day. He gave it a new exterior and as he saw it, repaired the omissions of the past. That may not be the opinion of modern archaeologists but we cannot blame him for not sharing the ideals of the late nineteenth and twentieth centuries, when we remember that in the first half of the last century there was serious talk of tearing down the Parthenon in Athens and replacing it with a pseudo-Gothic castle.

This remodelling of St. Sofia was but one of his many gifts to Kiev. He surrounded the old Pecherska Lavra with a stone wall. He repaired many of the old churches and even his enemies were compelled to admit that he was a patron of culture.

It was the same with the Kievo-Mohylanska Academy. He repaired the buildings. He called to its faculty scholars from Western Europe and increased the student body to over 2,000, drawn not only from all classes of Ukraine but from all the Orthodox lands of the Ottoman Empire and even from the Arab world. Under his Hetmanate it was easily the outstanding educational institution in Eastern Europe, even though it still retained too largely the ideals of a past century in its emphasis on rhetoric, philosophy and theology.

After his death, when there came a dispute over his property, his nephew Voynarovsky from memory compiled a list of some of his most important benefactions. Here are but a few of them.

"For gilding the domes of the Pecherska Lavra, 20,500 ducats; a wall around the Monastery and the Church, 1,000,000; a great bell and campanile for the Monastery, 73,000 zloty; a great silver candlestick for the Church, 2,000 imperials; a gold chalice and a mounting for the Gospels, 2,400 ducats; a gold mitre, 3,000 ducats, together with adornments and gifts for the Church; the gilding of the domes of the Metropolitan Cathedral in Kiev (St. Sofia), 5,000 ducats; a gold chalice for it, 5,000 ducats; its restoration, 50,000 zloty; the Church of the Kiev College with the gymnasia, etc., more than 200,000 zloty; the Church of St. Nicholas of Kiev within the Monastery, more than 100,000 zloty; the restoration of the Church of the Monastery of St. Cyril near Kiev, more than 10,000 zloty; an altar in the Monastery of Mezhihirye, 10,000 zloty; the foundation of a newly established Cathedral in Pereyaslav with a Monastery, also more than 300,000 zloty; the Church in Hlukhiv, 20,000 zloty; the refectory of the Monastery in Hustyn, 10,000 zloty; the refectory of the Mzharsky Monastery, more than 8,000 zloty; the Church of the Holy Trinity in Baturyn, 20,000 zloty; the unfinished Church of St. Nicholas in Baturyn, 4,000 zloty; the Monastery Church in Dihtary, 15,000 zloty; the Monasteries of Bakhmach, Kamyanets, Lyubets, Dumnitsya with their Churches, amount unknown; restoration of the Cathedral in Chernyhiv, 20,000 zloty; the completion of the Church of the Holy Trinity in that city, 10,000 zloty; the Makoshiynsky Monastery with the Church there, more than 20,000 zloty; for the restoration of the Monastery of St. Sava in Serbia he gave in Baturyn to the Archimandrite, the later Patriarch, 50,000 zloty; and for the completion of the building of this monastery and for other places in Palestine, 30,000 ducats to the Patriarch; a chalice of pure gold, a lamp and a silver altar for the Grave of our Lord in Jerusalem, 20,000 zloty; a silver shrine with five silver candlesticks for the relics of St. Barbara, 4,000 imperials; an altar for a Church in Wilno, 10,000 zloty; aid for the Orthodox to Bishop

Zhabokritsky of Lutsk, 3,000 zloty; a Gospel in the Arabic language for the Patriarch of Alexandria, 3,000 zloty and for him 5,000 zloty; in wooden churches: the Church of St. John the Evangelist in Chernyhiv with an altar, more than 8,000 zloty; two in Baturyn, the Resurrection and the Repose of the Mother of God, with their appurtenances, more than 15,000 zloty; in the village of Pracha, 15,000 zloty; the Church of St. John the Baptist in Rylsko 2,000 zloty."

This list does not include the offerings of Mazeppa to monasteries, churches, metropolitans, archbishops, bishops, archimandrites and other clergy in Greece, Palestine, Moldavia, Wallachia, Serbia, Bulgaria, Poland and Lithuania, to strangers in Ukraine, prominent clergy, various churches, monasteries, monks, students and soldiers. Each year Mazeppa also gave 1,000 zloty for the students in Kiev and 500 zloty to the Hustynsky Monastery.

These donations at their then value would total over a million dollars in our present money. When we multiply this to form an estimate of the purchasing power of these gifts at that time, we must pause to wonder at the liberality of the great Hetman. He was one of the great benefactors of his age, one of those men who have appeared in history as true patrons of art and the Church and we can understand why his name is still mentioned with admiration in many foundations outside of his native land. His bounteous gifts were not confined to Ukraine but they aided all the branches of the Orthodox Church in the Polish Republic and the entire length and breadth of the Ottoman Empire which at that time controlled all the Orthodox except those under Moscow. To those he gave far less. That was the province of the Tsars, but the Orthodox Christians in the Balkans, in Palestine and elsewhere had occasion to thank God for the aid which they received from the Hetman of Ukraine and the Christian foundations of the Holy Land still pray for the repose of his soul.

These donations were for charity. They do not include the enormous sums that he gave to Peter, to his courtiers, to every one in Moscow and the Muscovite service that could advance his cause and that of the Zaporozhian Host. That was political liberality that he used as a gilded weapon to secure himself against the plots of his enemies. It omits also the sums that he gave to his friends and supporters in Ukraine to assure their loyalty. He knew well that no one could outbid him and he acted accordingly.

His architectural style, the Mazeppa Baroque, was so skillfully handled by the native architects and the artists whom he hired from abroad that the Muscovites could do little better than employ the same men, if they wished to erect any monument or memorial and the Moscow Baroque as they called it was in far too many cases only a continuation by the same artists of the work of Ivan Mazeppa.

Architecture was not his only care. Painters and workers in the graphic arts swarmed to Kiev and Baturyn and found a ready welcome. In almost every field, except perhaps sculpture which was frowned upon by Orthodox tradition, the period of Mazeppa marked the golden age of Ukrainian culture. This included music, for the Brotherhood Chorus in Lviv in 1697 had in their library 267 works of known Ukrainian composers. Not since the early Grand Princes of Kiev had the financial wealth of Ukraine been in the hands of a man who knew so well how to use it for the development of the artistic side of his country.

Mazeppa had that love and appreciation of art that characterized the Italian princes of the Renaissance and which was in a sense embodied in King Louis XIV of France. His love of art was only part of that cultural atmosphere which he fostered, for he was not one of those patrons of art who are satisfied by donations of money.

He took a personal interest and in his yearly visits to the Kiev Academy, he was never weary of listening to the stilted and formal oratory of the students, their prolonged panegyrics and the exotic and artificial drama which the school cultivated. It was in his honor that Teofan Prokopovych prepared the first imitation of a tragedy, *Volodymyr,* in commemoration of the conversion of Kiev to Christianity.

Mazeppa never outgrew his interest in the Latin authors. He had become acquainted especially with the Roman historians and he hardly ever made a formal speech without referring to them. It gave his style a somewhat pedantic air but his Latin orations won the approval of all who heard him and not only of sycophants and flatterers.

It is the more remarkable therefore that with his broad interests he remained completely deaf to the progress of the contemporary knowledge and tendencies. Himself the author of several poems and of at least one duma in the traditional Ukrainian style, he was perfectly content to use throughout his life that artificial form of Church Slavic that was at once the protection of the Orthodox and the bar to the development of Ukrainian literature. There is not a sign that the Hetman gave the slightest attention to the possibility of writing in the vernacular. This is the more unusual, because he was well aware of the tendency in Moscow to abandon Church Slavic for the colloquial Russian of the day. He realized that Polish had found an aristocratic role beside the ecclesiastical Latin. He knew and spoke several European languages. Yet he clung stubbornly to the idea that the literary vehicle of the Kozak Host should be the Church Slavic even though in many ways he followed the traditions of the Kiev Academy and the Western tradition rather than the austere literalness of the School of Mount Athos.

It made Mazeppa a true product of the Ukrainian cultural revival which from its beginning had been pitched on a religious rather than on a national key. The brotherhoods in the sixteenth century, Petro Mohyla himself and now Mazeppa as the flowering of the movement, were content to remain within a circle which emphasized contact with the West through Poland but which by its vague and conservative tendencies played into the hands of Moscow as another Orthodox state.

Mazeppa thus left himself open to contradictory attacks. To the more bigoted Orthodox, he seemed a dangerous innovator in the field of culture. It was possible with a certain degree of fairness for his enemies to spread rumors that he was at heart interested in bringing Ukraine and the Host back under Polish control for he was devoted to the innovations that had come from there and violated the old Ukrainian traditions.

The group who saw his work only in political terms called him pro-Muscovite. He was encouraging many of the more talented young men to take service under the Tsars. He was emphasizing Orthodoxy as the factor for unifying the country and thus the transfer of the Church to the supervision of the Patriarch of Moscow meant the strengthening of those tendencies which were increasing the power of Moscow even in his own capital.

In all this he was again the direct opposite of Peter who in practical matters had turned aside from the entire past to admire uncritically everything that he could secure from the West, particularly Germany, and who was plainly inclined to use both Orthodoxy and culture as weapons to advance his own prestige, to weaken all the conservative sides of Russian society and to emerge with one vestige of the past, and one only, the autocratic character of the Russian Tsar.

Yet both friend and foe agreed upon the political and cultural significance of the Hetman. He was the final flowering of the Kiev Academy and the Kozak tradition and as he approached his seventieth birthday he was a distinguished character of the old school, moving like an Olympian through life and enjoying to the last drop all that it offered both of good and bad. He was the culmination of his period, the product of the Kozak Host, the Polish court, and his Muscovite friends, the subject of bitter attacks and the trusted companion of Peter when the latter returned from Europe and commenced to force the thorough Westernization of Moscow under his own autocracy, whether the people wished it or not.

CHAPTER ELEVEN

THE END OF THE CENTURY

The seventeenth century was drawing to a close and in 1699, Mazeppa, at the age of sixty seven, had already been for ten years Hetman of Ukraine. That was a long period, longer than the rule of Khmelnytsky, longer than any other Hetman except Samoylovych. Mazeppa was still alert and strong and to his friends and enemies he gave no sign of advancing age.

Fate had indeed been kind to him since he had crossed the Dnieper a quarter of a century before. He had risen steadily in power and wealth. He had reached a commanding position and he had been able to carry out his dream of reviving the culture of his country, in creating a new political system and cementing his own power.

Yet he could not help but feel the failure in his family life. His wife still lived on her colorless existence and never appeared at his court in Baturyn. He had no children. His aged mother, the Abbess Mary Magdalen, still governed her convent in Kiev, still visited Moscow periodically, still kept in touch with her son and gave him sound advice, when he needed it, on political as well as religious matters. His sister Oleksandra was dead after her hard matrimonial experiences.

All that he had left were his two nephews, the sons of Oleksandra, and he was doing his best to bring them up in his own traditions. The elder, Ivan Obidovsky, had been a receptive student. He had been graduated from the Academy of Kiev and the Hetman had attended the exercises that marked the graduation of the young man. Then he had entered the military service of the Host and had shown himself a competent leader and at the age of twenty he had received from his uncle the rank of Colonel, despite the opposition of the officers who complained at this sign of honor for the Hetman's nephew. Later Ivan had married Hanna, the daughter of Colonel Kochubey, the Chief Judge of the Kozak Host. Both men had welcomed this marriage, for Kochubey had been one of Mazeppa's oldest friends. The two had served together with Doroshenko across the Dnieper. The Hetman had helped and enriched his old friend and now by this marriage the relationship between the two men had become even closer. In fact this was not the only bond for Mazeppa had acted as godfather to Kochubey's youngest daughter Motrya.

The younger nephew, the half-brother of Ivan, Andri-Stanislav Voynarovsky, was still studying in Kiev. He had many of the intellectual tastes of his uncle. He appreciated far more than Obidovsky the cultural aims of the Hetman but he gave no signs of enjoying the political and military aspects of Mazeppa's life. He was obviously more artistic but it was not certain whether this concealed any physical or moral weakness, even though he was perhaps less suited for a high official position or the rank of colonel in a Kozak regiment.

Yet what of Ukraine? The country was still divided along the line of the Dnieper. The area over which Mazeppa had control was still bound hand and foot to Moscow. Mazeppa shuddered when he remembered the high hopes that he had had when he entered the Polish service. He had dreamed then of Ukraine as a region co-equal with the Poles and Lithuanians in the Polish Republic. He had failed. He had worked to make it an independent, even if neutral state, and he had seen the sad fate which had stopped this and had led to his transfer across the Dnieper. Now he had the state in hand but he was still unable to move without the will of the Tsar. He had no power of independent action and the Hetman, while he still maintained his position of independence, was fully conscious of the basic weakness of his position. He knew the discontent among the peasants who dreamed of the old independent life of the Kozaks and told tales and sang songs of the times when the Kozaks were a law unto themselves. The Kozak officers had become almost for them the equivalents of the old Polish landlords but they knew the uselessness of revolt. Even the men of the Zaporozhian Sich no longer were able to stir. Mazeppa still believed that he was really the captain of the ship; he still believed in a united Ukraine; he still called himself Hetman of both sides of the Dnieper, but he could not delude himself and he knew that any blow for freedom was useless and that the all-powerful Tsar Peter could bar any independent action on his part.

Peter had returned from his European trip in 1698 and he had come back more autocratic than ever. He had returned with a wild desire to westernize his country and do it over night. He had begun to change all the old established traditions, whether they were good or bad, and the conservative classes were calling him Antichrist and applying to him secretly worse epithets than Mazeppa had ever heard when he first came into contact with the haughty groups around Golitsyn and the old streltsy, but they dared not resist Peter's whims.

Peter was surrounded by a group of cultural upstarts. The chief of these was Menshikov, the ex-pastry hawker, the first member of the Order of St. Andrew and a man of no inherent culture, hardly able to read or write. A few of the old boyars still remained but their influence was steadily dropping and the court now reflected only the coarser and more plebeian forms of European life, while the Tsar in the most grotesque and vulgar ways sought to introduce his conceptions of Western culture. Only one thing had not changed, the power and ambitions of the Tsar and his autocratic control of the entire life of the country. His ruthless execution of the streltsy with his own hand had proved to the Muscovites that he was indeed a Russian Tsar worthy of the traditions of Ivan the Terrible and for those who doubted, the scaffolds in Moscow and the torture chambers of Preobrazhenskoye could convince them of the opposite. All this promised ill for Ukraine.

Yet what could Mazeppa do? Where could he hope to find allies or even friends? Mazeppa could be glad that he had not listened to the blandishments of King Jan Sobieski ten years before, for after the death of that sovereign, the Polish throne had been offered to the highest bidder. The French and the Empire had competed and the throne had been secured in 1696 by the dissolute Augustus II of Saxony, who considered Poland merely as a source of income for his court in Dresden. He moved a Saxon army into the country and tyrannized over it, so far as his love of pleasure and his drunken orgies would permit. The Poles were determined to have peace at all costs and were willing to submit to any foreign interference, any ravaging by hostile armies, so long as they were not compelled to fight in their own defence and were allowed to form their impotent confederations against the regime and to maintain their liberum veto whereby one man could prevent the adoption of any policy on any subject. The only agreement that existed was their continued opposition to the Kozak regiments, the Ukrainian population and the Orthodox Church. The Orthodox had almost disappeared from Lviv and the other cities under Polish control and the colonels of the Kozak regiments revived by Sobieski had no political or social rank. The situation was far worse than it had been in Mazeppa's youth and he could at least be thankful that he had not plunged the Ukrainians further into that tragedy.

What of Turkey? After the Turkish defeat at Vienna and the victories of Prince Eugene of Savoy on the Danube, the Turkish tide had ebbed. Peter's victory at Azov had checked the Khan of the Crimea and the Moslem world no longer had the power to interfere even in the case of a decadent Poland. There was nothing there to be hoped for.

And Sweden? The aid of Sweden had been the goal for which Khmelnytsky and Vyhovsky had been striving, for Sweden held a large part of the eastern Baltic shore and for decades Swedish envoys had been visiting the Host on various pretexts. Now all was changed. King Charles XI who had adopted a policy of peace and abandoned his claims to the Polish throne was dead and in 1697 the throne had been taken by an untried boy of seventeen, Charles XII, who had the confidence of no one at home or abroad.

Ukraine was isolated and as Mazeppa became conscious of his increasing age, he could see no hope for his country. He was already beginning to realize that he might be the last Hetman in the grand style. With all of his confidence, he could not be sure that after his death the Tsar might not see fit to make sweeping changes and to take actions that could only redound to the harm of Ukraine and the undoing of his own work.

Then as the century ended, everything changed. A strange series of intrigues commenced. A Livonian landowner named Johann Reinhold Patkul, angered at Sweden because it had questioned his ownership of some of his estates and had taxed them, appeared in Poland to beg Augustus II to form an alliance to seize the Swedish lands south of the Gulf of Finland and annex them. He found Augustus in a favorable mood. He had induced Denmark to cooperate but since he could not involve Brandenburg, he went to Moscow and appealed to Peter to join the confederation. Peter too took the bait and made peace with Turkey, for he was more convinced than ever that he could finally secure victory over the Khan without too much assistance from the Kozaks. Patkul had a second reason to involve Peter, for Peter had married his half-niece and half-nephew into the princely family of Gottorp, one of the areas that Denmark wanted to recover from Swedish overlordship in the neighborhood of Holstein.

A game of treachery followed. Peter renewed his peace treaties with Sweden at the very time when he was signing this alliance. Poland opened negotiations with Sweden against Russia at the same time. The nations of Western Europe were likewise making alliances and counter-alliances in connection with the succession to the Spanish crown. To Mazeppa it must have seemed as if the world had gone completely insane.

Suddenly early in 1700 the storm broke. The young Charles XII, wearied by the duplicity of his neighbors, suddenly led his armies into Denmark and to the amazement of Europe, he forced Denmark to sue for peace in three months. He had showed himself a master of military strategy. Then he turned on Augustus II who had sent a Saxon army to seize Riga and effectively defeated him.

Before all this news reached Moscow, Peter had almost casually moved an army to the north and was endeavoring to take the city of Narva. He had no doubt of success and was sure that Augustus could take Riga with no more difficulty. Along with this the Polish Diet declared its neutrality and refused to allow its army to fight on the side of its own elected King, so that the Poles paid no attention when the conflicting forces entered their territory.

These sudden developments almost over night changed the entire situation. Once again the positions of the countries involved was what it had been almost a century earlier. An embattled Sweden was fighting both Poland and Moscow and Moscow had never yet come into conflict with a major European state. Once again Western Europe was involved in a major war, that of the Spanish succession.

The chief difference was the lack of a clearcut religious issue. The Protestant Swedes were fighting Catholic Poles, Protestant Danes and Orthodox Russians. It was a political and not a religious or even a dynastic struggle and the prize was the control of the Baltic.

After twelve years of relatively clear sailing during which time Mazeppa's only possible move was to defend the interests of the Host against the constantly growing pressure exerted by Moscow, the aging Hetman was forced to take account of a situation which might result in great changes in the map of Europe. He was too old and cautious to take any rash action but the possibilities for alliances and counter-alliances were startling in the extreme.

Ukraine was in an ambiguous position. It was bound to Moscow and there were Muscovite garrisons in nearly all the important Ukrainian cities. Moscow and Poland were again allies but it was obvious that now Moscow was the stronger power and that in the long run Augustus II would be but a pawn in the hands of Peter. Sweden was the natural ally but despite his early victories Charles

XII was still relatively untried and the Hetman had no proof that in the game of treachery which had preceded the outbreak of hostilities, Charles would feel any interest in defending Ukraine, if he approached him with any promises. A false move would certainly make him lose his contacts with Peter which had been on the whole profitable to Ukraine and to himself and might lead to an ending of the privileges of the Zaporozhian Host. The prospects were terrifying and Mazeppa at sixty eight was in no mood to risk everything on one wild throw. He decided to support Peter and see what would happen.

CHAPTER TWELVE

MAZEPPA AND WESTERN UKRAINE

The Northern War had come as a thunderbolt to Mazeppa and to all the Zaporozhian Host. Yet at the very beginning Mazeppa remained true to the habits of many years. Whatever may have been the secret dreams that he cherished in his heart, he could not believe that Charles XII would be able to hold out long against the forces of Russia, Poland and Denmark and even the early victory over Denmark and the failure of the Poles to dislodge the Swedes from Riga did not serve to shake the confidence that the Hetman really felt in Peter. He personally had never had any experience with the attack of a modern army and he was perhaps in some degree critical of the new tactics that Charles was applying.

He was aware that Peter had changed and not for the better. His old love of dissipation had not been removed by his trip to Western Europe but his absence from his native land where he could rage at will had stored up a mass of savagery which was scarcely counterbalanced by his inordinate affection for all that he had learned and his indiscriminate admiration for all that he had seen. His vanity had ascribed to his new army the entire cause of the victory over the Tatars at Azov and it never occurred to him that his success might have been a combination of the new and the old. He confidently believed that Russian dignity plus a group of foreign officers made him the superior of anything that could be put into the field. At the same time both Gordon and Lefort were dead and they were the two men that he was willing to listen to from force of habit.

The Tsar hurriedly raised an untrained army of 50,000 men and hurried to Narva. In the very beginning of hostilities he had ordered Mazeppa to send some Kozaks to Livonia to assist Augustus. This was a volunteer force under the command of Colonel Iskra, as Appointed Hetman, but the force had scarcely been recruited when

Peter countermanded the order. Then at the first sign of real opposition he changed his mind and before the force was disbanded, he ordered the Hetman to send him 10,000 men. Again he changed his plans and countermanded his order. No sooner was this force demobilized than there came again a change and he called for 12,000 Kozaks whom Mazeppa sent under the command of his nephew, Colonel Obidovsky, and this force was in Pskov when the battle of Narva took place.

These sudden changes of orders began to alarm the Hetman. Under the terms of the alliance between the Host and Moscow, the Kozaks were not obliged to serve in distant lands. There might have been a question about the first order, for in peace or war the Host had always had a special attitude toward Poland and there might have been doubt as to whether they could rightly make this journey, for up to this time the Kozaks had only been employed in the warfare against the Turks, Tatars and Poles.

Mazeppa knew Peter too well to believe that the Tsar in a moment of crisis would stand strictly on the letter of the articles and he was not willing to raise the point, for he was beginning to see the real strength of Charles XII, even though he was not too conscious of its elements. He summarized his feelings in the beginning in a letter to Golovkin: "I would like to serve our great Sovereign and go where his Majesty is; then the army with the Hetman would maintain discipline and in the military operations the Kozaks would show still greater courage; but let it be as our very wise and all-seeing Monarch wishes. I shall be where his Tsarist Majesty wishes to have me."

Is this to be read as irony? When we remember the close relations that had existed for ten years between Tsar and Hetman we may doubt it, but there is undoubtedly a note of anxiety in view of the many changes of orders. These might seem a portent of danger to the discipline and order of the Host. At least they indicated that Peter was in some sense disturbed at bringing the Kozaks with their lack of European military discipline into contact with the Tsar's newly trained troops and his new officers. Mazeppa somehow felt that something was wrong and he began almost from the first days to wonder what that something was but he had scarcely made his mind up to any definite answer.

The battle of Narva on November 20, 1700 showed the truth of the situation. Instead of surrendering peaceably as Peter had expected, the Swedish garrison held out until Charles XII with 8,000 men could advance to its rescue. In the middle of a blinding snowstorm, he drove straight through the Muscovite lines. In the confusion, the troops believed that they had been betrayed by their foreign officers and attacked them. The entire Russian army disintegrated in a hopeless rout with Peter running faster and further than the rest. Only his two crack regiments, the Preobrazhensky and the Semenovsky, maintained any kind of order. Many of the foreign mercenaries who escaped alive from their own men were only too glad to seek the protection of Charles against a renewed outburst of savagery.

While the Kozaks were at Pskov, Colonel Obidovsky died suddenly. This was a severe blow to Mazeppa, for he had apparently dreamed of making the post of Hetman hereditary so as to avoid the confusion that always attended elections and Obidovsky was the only person to whom he could bequeath the post with any chance of his proving satisfactory, for he had no hopes that Voynarovsky with his artistic temperament would be able to exercise control.

What was worse in the eyes of the Hetman and the colonels was the contempt which the Muscovites and the foreign officers poured out upon the Kozaks. Peter's hesitation had apparently been caused by a shame at using these really irregular troops along with his new army, now that the battle was exposed to the eyes of Europe. The foreign officers who had never been in the steppes saw no value in these horsemen. Even as cavalry they were not to be judged by European standards and the foreigners were not slow in expressing their opinion. Naturally the Muscovites were only too ready to follow their example. They wanted to win Peter's approval by following the Tsar's foreign protégés and they were also able to vent their own national contempt for Kiev and all that went with it. This first encounter aroused the anger of the Kozak officers, even those most under Muscovite influence and they were not slow in reporting their anger to the Hetman.

This was but the beginning. The Russian defeat left the initiative fully in the hands of Charles and no one knew where he would attack next. The young monarch kept his own counsel. He not only concealed his moves and his plans from the enemy but also from his own officers. He planned his campaigns himself and then ordered his staff to prepare the technical details without informing them of his general purpose. No one knew when a march started, in which direction it was going or what was its destination. This was Charles' strength and weakness as a commander; his strength, because by no possible means could the enemy learn his plans; his weakness, because it discouraged his commanders from even speculating on or studying his tactics, so that they could apply them themselves in case of need.

Peter frantically sought to fortify the northwestern boundary of his country. Then he discovered that Charles had gone into winter quarters at Dorpat (Tartu) and in the spring of 1701 he turned against Augustus II of Poland. This gave Peter a welcome respite, for it allowed him to reorganize his shattered forces, to secure arms and ammunition from abroad and to make preparations for another campaign. He was confident of final victory but he still expected his Saxon-Polish ally to conquer Riga. It was therefore disconcerting to find that the King was attacking the interior of Poland and that Augustus would not give him any real assistance.

He finally decided to move on his own account and get control of at least part of the Neva River. For this, he ordered five regiments of Kozaks to leave Ukraine. Mazeppa, a little disturbed at the Tsar's methods, sent them under the command of Colonel Danylo Apostol, one of his most respected and trusted officers. The Muscovites and Kozaks raided extensively in Livonia and cleared the countryside of the Swedish forces but they made little impression upon the fortified towns. Still their victories over small

Swedish detachments gave them the upper hand in the country and allowed them to vent their anger on the helpless inhabitants.

Then the events at Pskov were repeated. The foreign officers in Peter's army made the Kozaks and their officers the object of derision and criticism. The force was ridiculed and abused. They were deprived of their proper share of the booty on the ground that they were not regular members of the Muscovite army. Muscovite and foreigner alike began to hint that the time was coming when the entire Kozak force would be remodelled on Western patterns. This was a thinly veiled way of saying that Peter had already conceived the idea of abolishing the Zaporozhian Host and of incorporating the whole of eastern Ukraine into the Moscow realm. There were constant threats that Peter would issue orders to turn the Kozaks into infantry and take away their horses and thus reduce them to an inferior status at the very time when the cavalry was considered the socially superior army of the service.

For warfare in the west there was some sense in all this and it should have sunk into the mind of Mazeppa. It should have been the signal for him to think of westernizing the tactics of at least part of his force. Yet he did not see it. He saw only an infringement of the rights of the Zaporozhian Host and his officers, with the same point of view, began to shower the Hetman with protests against the Muscovite high command and even the Tsar.

Their open murmuring was something new, something which he had not heard, since he had been Hetman. He knew the grumbling of the Kozaks. He knew the intrigues of the officers but he discounted them because he had given the officers large estates and the various Kozak factions had always been devoted to the conception of the Orthodox Tsar. He had long had to be on his guard against the attempts to slander him to the Tsar but he was a good enough judge of human nature to realize that at this moment the officers themselves were turning against the Tsar. Peter by his actions was actually fomenting that sentiment of Kozak nationality which the Poles had fanned before the time of Khmelnytsky and which apparently had largely disappeared during the past half century.

Mazeppa was aware that a different kind of crisis was impending but he could not at first determine its precise nature and its possible outcome. The officers were trying to protect their rank and their dignity, even if they were not thinking in terms of a free Ukraine. The Hetman had to find a solution for Ukraine or see himself become a wealthy Muscovite nobleman with his riches still intact but without any political position. This was a strange thought for the seventy year old Hetman and it bothered him more than he would admit.

As Charles won victory after victory and weakened Poland more and more, Peter decided that he would keep Augustus on his throne. Both Mazeppa and his officers had always dreamed of the time when they could recover for the Host the west bank of the Dnieper. Now they saw Peter trying to bribe the Poles to support and help their Saxon King by promising to maintain their control over that Ukrainian area. Finally Mazeppa ventured to complain to Peter: "It is dangerous to be friendly with the Poles. Our chroniclers have always written: 'While the world exists, a Pole can never be the brother of a Ukrainian.' It is true today." Mazeppa was not speaking from injured ambition but from his own experiences as a former Polish courtier.

Peter did not get angry and for the moment he seemed to yield. He sent a secretary to inform the Hetman that he would take no steps in this direction without consulting him. Mazeppa accepted this statement in good faith and without discussing the matter further, he shifted his policy to agree with that of Peter and for the moment tried to forget the dangers that faced the Host in the future.

Meanwhile Charles continued his campaign against Augustus. Early in 1702 from a position in Lithuania, he declared that the Elector of Saxony, a sarcastic allusion to Augustus, had forfeited the Polish crown and by the middle of August he had seized both

Warsaw and Krakow, while Augustus showed that he had no taste for continuing this struggle.

During this entire period, the situation in Poland grew more and more equivocal. The Poles persisted in their policy of official neutrality, even though the Swedish armies moved across their territory in search of the Saxon armies of their King and ravaged as well.

The Poles continued their policy of forming confederations, groups of local nobles who under the guise of taking sides for or against their King confined their attention to venting their personal hatreds against one another. In the eastern part of the country on the Ukrainian lands, these confederations found their chief bond of union not in devotion to any ideal of Poland but in making life miserable for the native Ukrainian population and trying to tear down the rudiments of Kozak organization which Colonel Paly had formed with the aid and help of King Jan Sobiewski.

Under such conditions the Poles could not guard the bank of the Dnieper, their official boundary. The Kozaks crossed and re-crossed the river, begging Mazeppa to take them under his protection. Paly himself paid several visits to the Hetman at Baturyn. He was royally entertained with all of Mazeppa's hospitality but the Hetman explained that he could take no action officially, for Peter and Augustus were allies in the common cause of opposing Charles and the Swedes. Yet these polite disavowals of the possibility of help did not prevent considerable amounts of guns and ammunition from disappearing from the arsenals of Mazeppa and appearing in the hands of Paly's Kozaks.

The Ukrainians regarded Paly as the ideal type of Kozak. He maintained the old democratic principles of the Zaporozhian Sich and with all of his bravery, he cared little for the tasks of administration. He was primarily a military leader, fighting against superior odds with insufficient means and for this reason he became celebrated in popular legend. He was a worthy member of that fine tradition which had been started in the sixteenth century and was broken by Khmelnytsky, when he put himself at the head of a political state. To him there were only two alternatives, freedom without government or government without freedom. The Kozaks on the west bank of course looked to Mazeppa for support and help but they did not really sympathize with his administration of east bank Ukraine and they did not do all that they could to set up a control of their own region. They were the helpless tools of the Poles.

Thus the Kozaks under Polish rule were still in that same inchoate state which had already cost Ukraine the lives of so many of her bravest sons. It was a fit parallel to the anarchy that reigned among the Polish nobles and played an important part in the wreck of the Polish Republic. The Kozaks knew this but as Shevchenko declared later, Poland fell but her fall ruined the Kozaks and Shevchenko was born and reared on the west bank.

Again and again Mazeppa begged Peter earnestly for permission to send his troops across the river and add the Western Ukrainians to his domain. Peter as consistently refused on the ground that he and Augustus were allies. In reality there was more to this game than appeared and the explanation was that Peter had no desire to irritate any section of the Polish public for he was hoping that sooner or later if he maintained Augustus in power, he might himself be able to swallow up the whole of Poland. Since he had slight use for the Kozaks, the Ukrainian population and their unhappy fate made no impression upon him. He was content to let the situation simmer, no matter what the cost to the Kozaks or to any one else.

Charles was not satisfied with this state of affairs. He very soon began to cast around for another candidate for the Polish throne. His first choice, the son of King Jan Sobieski, soon fell into the hands of Augustus but Charles then looked for a new candidate and he found him in the person of Stanislaw Leszczynski, one of the lesser nobles. It was evident from the end of 1703 that Stanislaw was destined to become the candidate of Charles but even those Poles who were most opposed to the regime of Augustus, hesitated and it was not until the next year that a Diet could be brought together at Warsaw to go through the formality of an election and in 1705 Stanislaw was finally crowned as King under the protection of Swedish arms.

During all this time the Poles continued to put pressure upon Paly and the Kozaks continued to exist under frightful odds. The Poles argued that the Kozaks were allies of the Swedes, even though Paly himself had never thought of adopting that policy and was interested only in protecting his own people. Yet the rumor served its purpose.

Augustus appealed to Peter to use his power and influence to suppress the Kozaks and once again the Tsar ordered Mazeppa to urge Paly to submit to the legal King. Mazeppa sent many messages "advising" Paly to do so but they were couched in such terms that Paly understood the Hetman's real meaning and declined. Finally when Peter insisted, Mazeppa answered in a tone that was unusual for him: "I cannot take the sin upon my soul and with proper certainty advise Paly, Samus and Iskra to obey and then give them over to the Poles to imprisonment. I cannot assure them that they will remain whole and not be injured both in their health and property. The Poles treat tyrannically not only the Kozaks but the entire Ukrainian population under their rule. Their recent actions along the Dniester and the Buh have shown this, where in vengeance for the uprisings of the people, they have punished many with death, hung them, thrown them on nails or pierced them with a spit."

Seeing that he could not move the stubborn Hetman in this case, Peter, as if he were the head of the Kozaks himself, ordered Paly to submit. Of course the Kozak leader refused and he was secretly supported by Mazeppa, who was still trying to find a way to get his own forces across the Dnieper and unify the country.

Duplicity was the order of the day and perhaps Paly, fighting against overwhelming odds, was the only direct actor in the picture. He was steadily driven from most of his haunts and finally appeared for a last stand in the neighborhood of Bila Tserkva. It is easy to imagine Mazeppa's feelings at the news that the last fights of the Kozaks were being carried on near his own birthplace. He knew the area thoroughly. All of his childhood memories were of this region and now he was unable to do more than send secret aid to the people among whom he had been brought up.

It was just at this moment that Augustus made another appeal to Peter and this time he begged for troops to allow him to put down the fighting around Bila Tserkva. In his plea he stated that the Poles there were his supporters and the Kozaks were the allies of Charles. This time the plea of Augustus was in a form that appealed to Peter and he ordered Mazeppa to lead his Kozaks across the river and place them under the orders of Augustus. To his surprise Mazeppa accepted at once. He did more than that. He gathered together the bulk of his forces, some 40,000 men, and led them himself to his birthplace.

As he crossed the Dnieper, Mazeppa glowed with satisfaction. For the first time in almost thirty years a Hetman was crossing the dividing line with the possibility of unifying Ukraine, for he was sure that he would receive the support of the Ukrainians of the west bank, now that there was no accepted Hetman there to oppose him. He saw himself doing what had not been done since the days of Khmelnytsky and he hoped to open in this way a new period in the life of Ukraine. His mother, the Abbess Mary Magdalen, was equally thrilled at her son's hope of recovering her old home and of wiping out or atoning for the long years of failure and disaster, before he had finally started his successful rise to power.

These were the dreams of Mazeppa and they were well within the range of possibility. They were at sharp variance with the definite orders that he had received from Peter, who regarded the crossing as merely a device to assist his friend Augustus at a difficult moment. Mazeppa knew those orders but he realized that Peter was always in search of new territory and he trusted to his own ingenuity and diplomatic skill to find some way of holding west bank Ukraine, once he had it under his control.

As he expected, he met with little opposition. The Kozaks and the Ukrainian population, after the years of Polish oppression, were only too glad to find a Ukrainian liberator. They cared little for the technicalities of the situation. They saw only the end of the nightmare that had plagued them for years and the possibility of an end to their oppression.

One unpleasant incident marked the occupation and to many people it seemed an act of treachery. On July 15, Paly visited Mazeppa and the men seemed to have arranged a final settlement. Mazeppa wrote secretly to Golovkin, Peter's Chancellor, that Samus had visited him and reported that Paly was preparing a council at Koshovaty and was hostile to him. On August 1, Mazeppa who had received in the meanwhile an order to arrest Paly, met him again and that night arrested him and when Mazeppa sent him to Peter, he was forwarded to Siberia. Peter still trusted Mazeppa and removed Paly from the picture. Mazeppa replaced him with a trusted officer of his own school, Colonel Omelchenko, who commenced to introduce the Hetman's system into the area as if he were in full control.

There is something peculiar in the entire episode. It aroused bitter criticism of the Hetman on the west bank for Paly had been very popular among the Ukrainians for his long, untiring struggle against their oppressors. Popular opinion and popular poetry were strongly in his favor and they both presented Mazeppa in an unflattering form. Even today the Kozak songs echo the feeling that it was wrong for a Ukrainian Hetman to hand over the champion of his people to the henchmen of the Tsar. It seemed to confirm the stories that Mazeppa was only a tool of Peter and it strengthened the distrust which he had won among the rank and file of the Kozaks.

It is hard to fathom Mazeppa's motives for he must have realized that it would be treated as an act of treachery and that he would receive the same kind of attack that he had felt years before when he was captured by the Zaporozhians on his mission to Turkey for Doroshenko. Yet we can see vaguely that there were real grounds for a deep hostility between the two men. The one was in the tradition of the Zaporozhian Sich; the other was trying to build up Ukraine and despised those Kozaks who refused to co-operate in forming an effective Ukrainian administration. Mazeppa was engaged in a trying business, for he was seeking to thwart the orders of the Tsar and he was apprehensive of what might happen, if an open fire of revolt in favor of Charles burst out on the west bank.

Peter obviously approved his attitude toward Paly but he was not a little disturbed at the overwhelming success of his Hetman. Mazeppa was too pro-Kozak, too little considerate of the feelings of the Poles and his actions tended to increase the spirit of Polish nationalism, not always in favor of Augustus. He might even succeed in creating such a storm among the Poles that they would reorganize themselves and thus end Peter's chances of getting complete control of the country through a puppet ruler.

Yet Peter did nothing. The war was not over. Charles was winning victory after victory. In the beginning Peter had expected that Augustus and the Poles would contribute their share to the common victory. Now with the insignificance of Augustus fully apparent, the Tsar saw that Moscow would have to carry the entire burden of victory. He wanted all of Poland but if that proved impossible, Mazeppa's policy might give him rich rewards. It might become a real asset, if worst came to worst. So he did not desire to reprimand the Hetman in whom he had an absolute trust.

He reiterated his orders that Mazeppa govern in the name of Augustus and the King confirmed his previous appeals that the Hetman punish the pro-Swedish nobles and Kozaks for their sympathies for Charles. Yet who were the guilty parties?

Mazeppa did not worry too much about the dilemna. He had orders from both the Tsar and the King to punish pro-Swedish Polish nobles and they were the men whom he had known as a child. In theory it was easy to distinguish the good and the bad. In practice it was a matter that required careful investigation and study but Mazeppa was required to produce immediate results.

He solved the problem in a very practical way out of his own experience. Those Polish nobles, whose families had been kind to him as a young man, he found ways and means of clearing. Those who had been hostile then were the representatives of Charles now. The Polish situation was so confused and the morale of both nobles and peasants so low, intrigue was so rife, that there was no one to question the decisions of the Hetman. The events of forty years before were now decisive. Long forgotten favors were remembered and long forgotten snubs and insults received their payment with interest.

For years Mazeppa had avoided his past, his failures and his disappointments. Just as he never spoke of his age and his past, so he never alluded to his past careers. Now at the end of his life he was back in his old home. Every village, every estate revived some memory and he was really rejuvenated when he returned to Baturyn on October 21, 1704 in triumph with his garrisons holding the west bank, even though they were nominally there as the representatives of his Royal Majesty, Augustus II of Poland.

CHAPTER THIRTEEN

AUTUMNAL LOVE

Mazeppa's wife died in 1702 as quietly and as unostentatiously as she had lived. Whether there was a lack of sympathy between the two or whether she was an invalid cannot be decided but from the time that Mazeppa entered the service of Samoylovych, she dropped completely out of sight. She did not appear at his entertainments; he apparently did not confide in her and she played no positive role in his life. She even did not appear in Moscow where Peter was trying to promote social life with his own crude tastes.

Like a gay bachelor, the Hetman went on his splendid way. He was noted for the beautiful ladies who surrounded him and affair succeeded affair. They were mere distractions of the moment, carried on as a pastime to wile away the hours or to bring the Hetman some political advantage. None of them were serious or involved him in any difficulties. His morals, if we may use such a term, were those of the pleasure-loving society of the day, which was anything but austere, no matter how devout.

Now just before he crossed the Dnieper in the spring of 1704, when he was somewhere over seventy, Mazeppa decided to marry again. It was as if the call to action and his return to his birthplace had roused in him long vanished hopes. He was no longer the tired and discouraged old man waiting for the end. He had some kind of idea that he might do something more for his country before he died and he wanted some one whom he loved to share his triumph. Perhaps some dream that he might still produce a son of his own came to him after the death of his nephew Obidovsky. Perhaps it was merely a burst of belated passion that led him to throw discretion to the winds and to risk for love the esteem of the Host and the confidence of the Tsar.

He suddenly approached Colonel Kochubey and asked for the hand of his daughter Motrya. She was the youngest child of

Kochubey and the most beautiful of his children, the sister of the girl who had married Obidovsky and she was still in her teens. There seems something peculiar in this love of the aged Hetman but Motrya reciprocated his feelings.

It was not the affair of a moment, a sudden outbreak and a sudden proposal to a comparative stranger. Kochubey was one of Mazeppa's oldest friends. The two men saw a great deal of each other both for personal reasons and because Kochubey was the Chief Judge of the Host. They were already bound together by the marriage of Obidovsky and Motrya's sister. Motrya was Mazeppa's godchild. As the little girl grew into womanhood, she had looked upon the Hetman as a second father and now that esteem had suddenly turned into ardent love.

No one had noticed this change in the situation. It could attract no attention in view of the close friendship that existed between her father and the Hetman. A constant visitor at the Kochubey home, he could not fail to meet the daughter and then as the friendship developed, no one realized that the presents the Hetman showered upon her were anything but a sign of confidence and friendship for the family. No one suspected that the two were seeking every chance of meeting secretly or that the girl would throw all discretion to the winds in her passion for the Hetman.

Colonel Kochubey was startled at the formal proposal of the Hetman for he had no idea of the situation. He appreciated the honor shown him but he realized that there were more than fifty years difference in the ages of the two and this was a terrible obstacle. The Hetman would not take no for an answer and Motrya was equally emphatic and insisted upon the marriage.

The mother was even more bitter. She was a strict and austere woman who had no desire to see her daughter in the arms of the Hetman who had had such a variety of amatory experiences. She bitterly berated both Mazeppa and her daughter and poured abuse upon her husband for even his hesitation in objecting to the proposed marriage.

The Church was on her side. Under Orthodox canon law, the marriage of godfather and godchild was strictly prohibited. It was regarded as incest exactly as if the two were father and daughter, for the Church taught that relation by baptism was as true and binding as any tie of relationship. This gave Madame Kochubey an exceptionally strong weapon against the marriage.

She did not hesitate to make the most of her position. She scolded and berated her daughter. She tried to persuade her of the error of her ways and then abused her roundly, when the girl persisted in her intentions. Finally she commenced to watch her. Motrya was not allowed out of the sight of her mother or her most trusted servants. She was shut up in the house and refused permission to go anywhere, lest she succeed in meeting the Hetman. In addition to that the mother took pains that the news of her daughter's infatuation should be made known to all the officers and their families.

This was the most unusual feature of the situation. Mazeppa was very obviously trying to save the girl's reputation, while he prosecuted his suit but Madame Kochubey seemed completely deaf and blind to the consequences of her unrestrained abuse and gossip. She did not think of her daughter's reputation and blackened it to her heart's desire. Perhaps she was already hoping to stir up a faction to overthrow the Hetman. If she was, she did not succeed but she did arouse deep hostility against herself and her husband.

Mazeppa ignored all the gossip. He did not allow it to interfere with his relations with his old friend. He was as kindly and gracious to the Kochubeys as in the past. He entertained them as ever and accepted their invitations. Of course Motrya was not present. Mazeppa may have hoped for a passing glance at his beloved, if only by accident, but he was too trained in the ways of the world to reveal his feelings at any of these visits to the Kochubeys.

The climax came one night. After an especially bitter scene with her mother, Motrya succeeded in escaping from the house. She fled late at night through the dark streets of Baturyn and took refuge in the palace of the Hetman. Madame Kochubey soon noticed her absence. She undoubtedly suspected where Motrya had gone but instead of sending quietly to the palace to bring the girl back, she induced her husband to ring the alarm bell and to rouse the city. Kochubey like a dutiful husband obeyed.

The alarm of course aroused Mazeppa. He immediately found Motrya and then to quiet suspicion, he sent for the representatives of the Tsar and asked them to take Motrya back to her home. This was a shrewd solution for it gave the Muscovite agents full opportunity to learn from Motrya in the absence of any of the Hetman's men whatever they wished to learn. Of course they were only too glad to do it and were thoroughly prepared to accept Mazeppa's and Motrya's version of the affair. Colonel Kochubey got his daughter back and all the tongues in Baturyn began to wag but under conditions where the Tsarist authorities were against Kochubey.

Madame Kochubey tried to spread the story that Mazeppa had kidnapped the girl by force and had kept her with him in the palace for a considerable time. There was no evidence of this and Mazeppa's version that he did not know of her presence in his palace until it was brought to his attention by the ringing of the alarm and that he had then taken immediate steps for her safety and return home could not be disputed.

Of course it is impossible to rule out the possibility that Motrya had escaped from her home to keep a definite date with the Hetman but it is equally possible that the Hetman was telling the truth and that the girl had been overwrought by family opposition and had risked everything on a mad escapade in the hope of finding refuge from an intolerable situation.

Even after this, Mazeppa did not give up his suit. He continued to write to Motrya and to send her valuable presents, even while he was across the Dnieper. At least a part of these were intercepted by Kochubey and ultimately found their way into the hands of Peter. There are no known replies from Motrya, although there are indications that Mazeppa received word from her. Perhaps she was unable to write him for her father and mother intercepted the letters. Perhaps Mazeppa received them and destroyed them or perhaps they perished along with his other documents.

Those letters that have survived show the Hetman in a strangely different light. They reflect a different side of his personality, that ardor and directness that marked his service to Jan Kazimierz at the Polish court. Perhaps he showed to Motrya his real self which he had kept hidden during his long and apparently cynical career. They are formal, yes, but not in that pedantic and turgid style natural to the scholar who was never weary of listening to long panegyrics in Latin and other languages and who stressed the tinsel and trappings of life. Here are some extracts from them.

I

My dear heart, my darling little rose,

I suffer in my whole being at the thought that you are far from me; I cannot see any more your eyes and your white face. I kiss and embrace you tenderly.

II

My dear heart,

I am so sad to learn from your servant that you are vexed with me, because I did not keep your Grace in my house and sent you back to your parents.

But think a little yourself what would have been the result.

First of all, your parents would have spread the story through the whole world that I had kidnapped their daughter by force (Note—they did) during the night and they would have claimed that I was keeping you as a mistress.

Finally in keeping your Grace neither you nor I would have known how to act. We would have been obliged to live as a newly married couple, while the blows of the Church and its curses would have forced us to separate. What would I have done then? Would I not have suffered, if your Grace had complained of me?

III

Love of my heart,

I beg you, I beg you earnestly to meet me. We have to talk. If you love me, do not forget me; if you do not love me, do not remember me. But remember your words. Did you not promise to love me and give me your white hand?

I repeat again a hundred times; I beg you, let me know where I can meet you for our mutual good fortune, if only for a single minute, as you promised me before. If it is impossible, take off your necklace, I beg you, and send it to me.

IV

My dear heart,

Your beautiful face and your promises have eaten me up. I am now sending to your Grace little Natasha to arrange with you all the details. Don't be afraid of her; she is devoted to you as she is to me. My dear heart, I embrace your little feet; I beg you, do not put off the fulfilment of your promise.

V

My well-beloved heart,

You know how I love you, with all my heart, like a mad man. Your Grace, I have never loved any one in the world this way. It would be my happiness and joy to see you come to live in my house. But I have asked myself what would be the end of all this, especially in view of the wickedness and obstinacy of your parents. I beg you, my heart, change nothing! Did you not often give me your word and your hand? For my part, as long as I have a breath of life, I will never forget you.

VI

My dear heart,

I have no news of the situation of your Grace. Have they stopped tormenting you and bothering you? I am going away for a week and am sending you this present on my departure through my servant Karl. I beg you to accept it and to keep your love for me unchanged.

VII

My dear heart,

How I suffer and still I cannot tell it myself in detail to your Grace or claim you in your present sorrow. Tell this girl what you think I have to do. Finally if your accursed parents disown you, take refuge in a convent and I will then know what I will have to do with you. I repeat it again, let me know what you want.

VIII

Love of my heart,

I have been terribly upset on learning that that wretch, your mother, has not stopped humiliating your Grace, as she did yesterday. I do not know what to do with that miserable woman. All the evil comes from the fact that I have had no good opportunity to talk to you a little in detail about all this. I cannot write any more. I have so much sorrow and vexation. If I could only talk to you. Whatever happens, as long as I live, I will love you with all my heart and will never stop wishing you well. I repeat it, I will never stop—to the confusion of your enemies and mine.

IX

Love of my heart,

I see that your Grace has completely changed her old love for me. You know it; let your will be done. Act as you wish. You will be sorry later. Remember only your word that you gave me under oath, when you left the palace, when you took from me a diamond ring, my most beautiful and costly jewel. You said then: "Whether it happens one way or another, our love will never die."

X

My dear heart,

Let God separate from His soul whoever tries to separate us.

Oh, I know how to take vengeance on my enemies but you have bound my hands.

It is with great sadness in my heart that I am waiting from your Grace news of the affair which you know yourself.

XI

Love of my heart, my darling, all-beloved little Motrya.

I expected to die rather than notice such a great change in your heart. Remember only your words, remember your oath. Look at your little hands; didn't you often give them to me and say, "Whether I am with you or not, I will love you till I die?" Didn't you promise it?

Remember finally our talk of love, when we were together in my apartments and talking.

"May God punish the unjust man!" you said. But whether you love me or not, I will never stop being faithful to my word and will love you till my death, to confound my enemies.

In any way at all, I beg and implore you, my dear heart, I must see you. I must talk with your Grace for I will not tolerate any longer the scheming of my enemies; I will pay them back by giving them the place they deserve. What is that? You will see for yourself.

My letters are happier than I; they are in your hands; they are happier than my poor eyes, for they cannot see you.

XII

Love of my heart, my darling little Motrya.

I salute your Grace, my dear heart, and in saluting you, I am sending you as a present this little book and this diamond ring. I ask you, think well about wearing it and keep your love faithfully for me until God permits me to announce to you something better.

I kiss your ruby lips, your white hands and all your white gleaming body, my adored beloved.

*   *   *

These letters do not sound like the missives of the all-powerful Hetman of Ukraine who for almost a half century had matched his wits and self-control against all contestants in the ruthless game of politics and had won. They sound like the vaporings of a lovesick youth who had met with obstacles in the courtship of his young sweetheart. They give us a clue to a personal side of Mazeppa and reveal something that he showed only to Motrya and his mother.

What could he have done? Peter had succeeded in placing his wife Eudoxia in her convent where she could not interrupt his plans and later, many years later he had married a woman of lesser birth who succeeded him as Catherine I. With Peter's help and perhaps with the aid of his mother, Abbess Mary Magdalen, he might have succeeded in removing the ecclesiastical obstacle by one device or another. But he could not do it, while the Kochubeys maintained their position. It would have been more rash and dangerous than his love and that was serious as it was.

Finally Kochubey presented a formal complaint to the Hetman about the unhappiness that his daughter had caused him and the disgrace that she had brought upon him. He did not attack Mazeppa by name but there was no mistaking the allusion.

Mazeppa answered in his cold and formal style and scathingly denounced Madame Kochubey, "an insolent and talkative woman who ought to be muzzled as a vicious horse." He blamed her for all of Kochubey's misfortunes and advised the colonel against listening to the words of such an empty-headed and evil woman. Then he took up the question of Motrya in a formal and religious style and preached a sermon, comparing her to various saints and Biblical characters. "Did not Saint Barbara flee from the house of her father Dioscurus and not to the palace of a Hetman but to a far more wretched place, the shelter of some shepherds?"

He concluded: "If some day your roof and your house perish, you will have no one to reproach; you can thank only the cursed insolence of your wife. As for the debauchery of which you speak in your diatribe, I do not know what you mean. Would it not refer to you yourself, if you listen so much to your wife?"

This seemed to settle the issue and there were no open repercussions. As far as any one could tell, it did not affect the relations of the two men. They continued to be the same bosom friends. They kept appearing in each other's company. Perhaps they avoided the troublesome subject and perhaps, as events showed, the concealed venom was doing its work in both. The ardor of Mazeppa seemed to cool and gradually his affection for Motrya was crowded into the background by other more dangerous developments.

For a while sentiment in Baturyn was divided. There were those who condemned the Hetman. They argued that he had seduced his goddaughter and that then he had thought up the idea of marrying her. The majority took his side and, however inadvisable they thought the marriage, they condemned the Kochubeys for their needless exposure of their unfortunate daughter to public obloquy.

The Kochubeys did not forget, especially the wife. They nurtured their hatred for the Hetman and sought only for an opportunity to injure him. Their chance soon seemed to come.

CHAPTER FOURTEEN

PLANS AND COUNTERPLANS

Despite his absorption with Motrya Kochubey, Mazeppa spent an active summer in 1704 across the Dnieper. He succeeded in bringing the greater part of the west bank under his control but its fate depended upon the future relations between Peter and Augustus for by their agreement at the same time Peter had again promised the area to Augustus. The actions of Charles XII were also important.

On his return to Baturyn in the autumn, Mazeppa found a new spirit. Both the officers and the ordinary Kozaks were roundly indignant at the treatment which they had received from the Russians, especially in the north, and they brought back very definite information that Peter was only waiting for an opportunity to wipe out the Zaporozhian Host and turn the Kozaks into dragoons or ordinary infantry.

It was only natural for Peter to adopt this attitude. He was so obsessed with his admiration for the West that he could not see that the Kozaks had specialized in warfare in the East against the Tatars and that he was using them for purposes for which they were not really fitted. He saw only that they were not Western cavalry and he lost no opportunity to sneer at them. His foreign officers, unfamiliar with the East and the steppes, followed the example of the Tsar.

In addition to this Peter had no use for any force which claimed traditional privileges and exemptions. He refused to understand that the Host had existed before it had come into contact with the Muscovites and that the officers were proud of their own traditions. He had ridden roughshod over the dearest ideas of his own people. He had compelled them to shave and wear European clothes and he saw no reason why he should respect the Kozak feelings. He could drink and carouse with Augustus of

Poland but he fundamentally despised him and used him only as a tool. He had long before made up his mind that he would settle the Kozak question by a sudden order but he was a little hesitant to do this while Charles was winning victory after victory and so he kept postponing a final decision.

The officers poured out their troubles to Mazeppa. The Hetman listened sympathetically but he said nothing. Officially he would not countenance their opinion. In fact he went so far as to write to Peter his regrets that he had heard officers venturing to criticize the Tsar. At the same time he took no steps to discipline the grumblers and it is not impossible that his secret agents even inspired some of it.

In January 1705, Mazeppa, the General Osaul Skoropadsky and five other officers visited Moscow. He was received royally. Peter was apparently still hesitating about his course in Poland. He did not reprimand the Hetman for the case of Paly or his other actions across the Dnieper. He was sure that whatever was afoot among the Kozaks, the Hetman was not a party to it and that he could rely upon his fidelity and loyalty as in the past.

Then Mazeppa in the summer recrossed the Dnieper to visit his new lands. It seemed to be necessary for the old Hetman to revisit the land of his youth, to live over his old memories and to recover there some of the ardor that he had had when he was young.

There was another reason. Mazeppa did not want to depend only upon his agents and representatives. He wanted to have a personal contact with the region for he knew the moods of the Polish magnates and the untrustworthiness of their sympathies. They were as subject to fits of passion as were the rank and file of his Kozaks. He had never seen such a bewildering series of events but he believed that he could find some clue through his personal relationships.

While he was there, Charles determined to settle the Polish question and on September 3 in Krakow he forced the coronation of his candidate Stanislaw Leszczynski in the traditional site on the

Wawel, the old fortress palace of Poland. He then moved into Saxony to compel Augustus to resign the throne, whether he would or not and whether he remained at the court of Peter or not. With Charles to think was to act and so with his army he started on a new campaign.

This singlemindedness, this power of concentration on one part of a situation was at once a strength and a weakness of Charles XII. He had dealt first with the King of Denmark and Denmark was out of the war. He had defeated Peter at Narva and elsewhere but he determined to treat Russia as the final enemy. Before that he was going to finish with Poland and Augustus. As a result his campaigns in Poland followed the traditional lines of the early Vasa kings and he gave no thought to such problems as Ukraine, the Zaporozhian Host and the southern neighbors of Poland. He thus gave Peter time to remodel his army and prepare to meet him.

The coronation of Stanislaw created a new feeling for Augustus. The Polish magnates, always jealous of their prerogatives, resented the pressure that was being exerted upon them and there came a perceptible reaction in favor of the former King. Stanislaw could be sure of only a little direct help from the Swedes and he knew himself to be only a Swedish puppet, and so he sought for some support that would give him a little freedom for movement. His choice, the traditional choice of the Polish Kings, was the Kozaks and with it the traditional Polish desire to control the whole of Ukraine.

He began to make efforts to get in touch with Mazeppa, for he was well aware of the attitude of the Kozak officers toward Peter. He sent the Hetman a Polish agent named Wolski to offer him an alliance, provided he would break with the Tsar. Mazeppa's action was typical. He seized Wolski and placed him under arrest. Then he forwarded the message to Peter and assured him that he would not bother with such proposals and he laughed at the idea that a puppet like Stanislaw could have any effect upon his loyalty. Yet by some extraordinary circumstance Wolski succeeded in making his escape from his guards as they were taking him from the Kozak camp.

Then Mazeppa met Princess Anna Dolska. She was an attractive lady of about fifty years of age and one of the outstanding figures of Polish society. As Princess Anna Chodorowska she had married at about the age of 14 in 1676 Prince Christof Koribut Wisniowiecki, a man some thirty years her senior. They had three children and she was left a widow in 1686. In 1689 she married Prince Jan Karl Dolski, the Grand Marshal of Lithuania. They had one son. Dolski died in 1695 and soon after her son by the second marriage. From that time she devoted herself to the education of her children by Wisniowiecki and to dabbling in Polish political life. Incidentally she was an aunt of Stanislaw Leszczynski whom she greatly admired, although she was openly a supporter of Augustus.

This does not tell the whole story. Her first husband, Prince Christof had been brought up by his uncle, the Terrible Jarema, the chief enemy of Khmelnytsky and the Kozaks. Still he was a member of that family, which, while it was still Orthodox, had been one of the founders of the Zaporozhian Sich and all the Wisniowieckis, despite their anti-Ukrainian attitude, had succeeded in keeping on friendly terms with many of the Kozak officers. Mazeppa himself as a young man had been very friendly with her first husband. He had spent the summer of 1663 with them. He knew intimately the estates and the traditions of the family and now in the mood that was coming over him, those memories gained strength.

It seems unlikely that Mazeppa had ever met her earlier but in November 1705, her son Janus Wisniowiecki visited the Hetman in his camp at Dubno and invited him to their estate at Bila Krynytsya to act as godfather for one of his daughters. Ostensibly because of his past relations with the family, the Hetman accepted. Naturally the grandmother was present. Ivan Mazeppa talked with her day and night for two whole days. The cynical wondered what they were discussing but there were no definite clues. Somewhat later Colonel Kochubey reported that she had offered the Hetman in the name of King Stanislaw the title of Prince of Chernyhiv, but he had no evidence to support his story.

Pylyp Orlyk himself did not know and Orlyk was now the most trusted aide of Mazeppa. His family was of Czech origin but he had early thrown his lot in with the Kozaks who cared little as to a man's racial origin. As an educated man, a graduate of the Kiev Academy, with a knowledge of Western Europe, Orlyk rose rapidly in the service of the Host and he was soon made General Secretary, the post that Mazeppa had held under Doroshenko. It made him the personal secretary of the Hetman and if there was any one who was familiar with Mazeppa's plans, it was Orlyk.

When Mazeppa returned to his camp, he asked Orlyk to send the Princess a note of thanks and he enclosed also a code in which she could correspond with him. That was all that Orlyk could learn at the time but the Princess answered almost at once and apparently a real friendship was formed on the basis of her first husband. More important than that she became the intermediary between the Hetman and King Stanislaw.

No one knew this at the time except perhaps Orlyk. Yet the friendship was not secret. There was nothing reprehensible about it, for Mazeppa's orders commanded him to be on good terms with the Poles loyal to Augustus and such the Princess claimed to be. Mazeppa was almost openly declaring his friends to be loyal to the King and his enemies friends of the Swedes but who was to decide in the confused state of Polish politics?

Still to make assurance doubly sure, Mazeppa reported the attempt to approach him to Peter just as he had in the case of Wolski and he mentioned several other attempts that had been made to win his favor for Stanislaw.

Meanwhile the anger of the Kozak officers continued to mount as more and more returned from campaigns with the Muscovite armies and reported newer and newer insults. Colonel Horlenko, for example, told how a Muscovite officer had seized his horse and then he demanded, "What do you as our leader think of all this?"

Mazeppa made the strange answer: "That is the reward for our services. I would like to see another man in my place. I am a fool for I have just rejected the proposals of Stanislaw." It gave the officers a hint that Mazeppa was planning something but it did not reveal the way in which his mind was working and he refused to explain his enigmatic remark.

In March, 1706, Peter ordered him to move with his armies to Minsk. At the time Charles was besieging in Grodno a large Muscovite army under General Ogilvy, who finally succeeded in disentangling his forces and retreated, laying the country waste behind him. Peter, discouraged over the course of the war, believed that Charles would undoubtedly next attack Kiev but Charles was not yet ready and he moved to Saxony to finish with Augustus.

At the same time Mazeppa received another letter from Princess Dolska. It had apparently been brought to him by a wandering monk. Orlyk deciphered it. It stated that the Princess had received a letter from a certain King and that detailed propositions would follow.

Did she refer to Charles or to Stanislaw? The difference is important in estimating the motives and the political acumen of the Hetman, for he only answered Orlyk, when he had finished the deciphering: "The crazy woman! She wants through me to deceive His Majesty so that he will abandon King Augustus and take Stanislaw under his protection and he promises such resources that it will be possible for His Majesty to defeat and conquer the Swede. I have spoken of her nonsense to the Tsar and he laughed at it."

Mazeppa was largely telling the truth, for at this stage of the campaign he kept Peter fully informed of all his movements or at least of all of which Orlyk was aware. Perhaps he had not yet made up his mind as to what course he was going to adopt. Perhaps his natural caution had been so increased by the years and the shock of the affair with Motrya that he was unable to come to any decision.

As Hetman of Ukraine and subject to the Tsar, he had succeeded in getting control of west bank Ukraine and he well knew that if Peter were to win only a partial success, he might be satisfied with annexing this part of the Polish state. In that case Mazeppa had gained much for Ukraine. The danger was that the Tsar was obviously intending to ignore all the rights of the Kozaks and to treat them as ordinary subjects. That might be a peril to the future of the Host for there were too many rumors that the Tsar intended to abolish the privileges of the entire organization in his desire for uniformity. It would affect him less personally; his life was nearly over and he felt certain that he could retain Peter's confidence to the end. But what of the future? He was loyal to the Host, he always had been, and he always would be.

King Stanislaw was obviously trying to establish some direct contact in the hope that he might win him and the Kozaks away from the Tsar. Did he really think that through Mazeppa he could win the support of Peter and thus cement his position by abandoning Charles? Either scheme promised no good for Ukraine. Mazeppa was too experienced in the ways of Polish politics to believe that for one moment the Polish magnates would ratify any promises made by the King in his hour of need. He had seen that before and as a matter of fact he had received no hint of an offer that had come anywhere equalling in importance that which he had carried for King Jan Kazimierz to Hetman Vyhovsky. An agreement between Peter and Stanislaw would merely increase the troubles of his country. It might offer the Kozaks a breathing spell but that was all. Peter would still find ways of carrying out his plans.

Yet it would never do to reject offhand any proposals of the King of Poland for behind them might lie the wishes of his backer, Charles XII of Sweden. Mazeppa knew how much weight the former Hetmans had laid upon a Swedish alliance. Following his custom, the Swedish King had apparently given no thought to the problem of Peter and Moscow. He had won a few victories and had then gone on in pursuit of Augustus. Neither through the Poles nor through his own agents abroad had Mazeppa been able to obtain even the slightest hint as to Charles' future plans and they were the all-important factor. The moment that the Hetman could be convinced that Stanislaw was honestly speaking for Charles, the situation would be radically changed.

Till that moment his best course was to remain loyal to Peter, to continue to encourage Stanislaw mildly and to wait and wait and wait. He realized the strain that this was going to put upon him, the drain on his failing strength, the almost superhuman patience that he would need, but he still had faith in himself and his own ability. With this in mind, he would allow his officers to have a free reign in their conversations, but at the same time he would satisfy to the last possible degree the legitimate or illegitimate demands of the Tsar.

In this he was consistent. He was the captain of the ship. He was the captain of the Kozak Host, that old ship which was now in such a dangerous position. It was his task to steer it and woe to the man or officer who interfered.

It was not long before the officers began to talk of the Treaty of Hadyach. Colonel Lomykovsky and Colonel Apostol actually secured the original text of the treaty and discussed it with their friends. Mazeppa carefully kept away from their meetings. In general terms he kept the Tsar posted but without betraying any one. He had no object in concealing it, for he was very sure that the Tsar's representative in Baturyn could not fail to notice and report the growing dissatisfaction of the higher officers.

From Minsk Mazeppa returned to Baturyn and then he went to Kiev, for Peter was coming there in the middle of the summer to inspect the new fortifications. The Tsar was sure that Charles was going to attack through Kiev when he left the north and so he hurriedly gave his orders.

These fortifications only added fuel to the fire. They were being built by foreign engineers with Muscovite overseers. The ordinary labor was furnished by the Kozaks who perished in large numbers because of the pace at which they were being driven. It was a kind of work that was repugnant to the Kozaks but Peter had the satisfaction of forcing them to do something without their horses and that was enough for him. He saw these works not only as a means of driving off Charles but of breaking the Kozak pride and self-respect.

Meanwhile Princess Dolska continued to bombard Mazeppa with letters written in their private code. She continued to make all kinds of promises in the name of King Stanislaw and she added vague hints that the Hetman in return would receive some form of guarantee from Charles who was now in Saxony. All in all these letters contained nothing that would have justified Mazeppa in changing his policy.

According to the story told by Orlyk, Mazeppa was in bed with the gout when one of them arrived. On hearing its contents, Mazeppa jumped up and exclaimed: "That accursed woman is crazy; she asked me once before to induce the Tsar to take Stanislaw under his protection and now she writes something else; the woman is mad, she wants to catch me, me, a tried and clever bird; it would certainly go bad for me, if I let myself be fooled by a woman; is it possible to leave the living to look for the dead or to leave one bank and not to reach the other? Stanislaw is not sure of his crown; the Republic is two-faced; what can be the basis for the mad promises of this woman? I have grown old, serving His Majesty and his father and brother faithfully. I was not led away by the Polish King Jan Sobieski, the Khan of the Crimea or the Don Cossacks; and now at the end of my life a woman wants to deceive me." He burned the letter and added: "Write a cipher letter to this woman at once, without leaving here: 'I ask your Princely Highness to stop this correspondence which can ruin me in my life, my honor and my property. Do not even hope or think that in my old age I will injure my fidelity to my Imperial Majesty which I have kept inviolate since my young years and in which I wish to die, for I do not want during my life and after my death to bring upon my person the shame and name of traitor and so I ask you again to cease this correspondence and not to write me again."

Orlyk wrote the letter as he was directed but there is no way of knowing whether Mazeppa sent it or not. It was some months before Orlyk knew of any more letters but that does not mean that Mazeppa really broke off his negotiations. It has often been conjectured that Mazeppa burst out to test the loyalty of his secretary but perhaps the Hetman had another object in view and that was to force the intervention of Charles himself as the vital factor in the situation.

It is hard to date these secret letters. The mention of the Don Cossacks makes it possible that this episode happened in 1707 for in that year Kondraty Bulavin, an ataman of the Don, rose in revolt, seized Astrakhan and raged up and down the lower Volga valley. Peter ordered Mazeppa to send forces against him and he did send a volunteer force which joined with Muscovite forces in suppressing him.

Many historians have criticized Mazeppa for doing this. They have argued that he should have made common cause with the rebels as a great democratic demonstration. This never occurred to Mazeppa and his officers. It was contrary to the principles and policy of the Host from the time of Khmelnytsky and this was not only due to the growth of aristocratic feelings among the officers. There was a latent feeling for real nationalism in the Host. Its leaders and its members were conscious that they were not Muscovites, that they had more Western connections. The Don Cossacks looked toward Asia and Iran. For a while in the preceding half century their great rebel Stenka Razin had actually taken refuge in Iran. The Don was aflame with Muscovite religious fanaticism, that form of Orthodoxy which looked askance at Kiev and its former relations with the Greeks and the Balkan peoples. The Don had appealed to Mazeppa but it was far closer in its political thinking to the Kozaks of the Sich than it was to the officers who were trying to maintain Western ideals as they understood them. It was useless for the Host to join the struggle for the

Old Faith and the Beard, the two slogans that had been used so effectively against the first Kievans in Moscow. However the revolt was finally suppressed and Bulavin was executed.

Meanwhile the European pot was boiling and both Peter and Mazeppa were intensely anxious. For nearly a year Charles remained in Saxony and his presence there also troubled the nations engaged in the War of the Spanish Succession. Sweden and France were traditional allies and England, the Empire and the other members of that coalition were mortally afraid that Charles would give up his own fight and join Louis XIV against them. The Duke of Marlborough, the foremost English general, even visited Charles at the Castle of Altranstädt to try to learn his feelings and he was overjoyed that the King showed no desire to interfere in the Western war.

The fear that he would was a nightmare to Mazeppa. He was visited by French agents who tried to persuade him to join Stanislaw and thus secure sufficient forces for the defeat of Peter without the need of the army of the Swedish King. Representatives of the coalition tried to persuade him to be true to Peter so as to keep Charles involved in the east. If Charles went west, Mazeppa knew very well that in the game of treachery which was being played all over Europe, it would throw Ukraine and the Host back to where it had been a century before. Poland, with Peter defeated, would have a chance to break its word. If it did not, it would arouse new internal conflicts among the Kozaks and then even a defeated Peter would be able to profit.

On the other hand Peter was equally alarmed. He wanted Charles to go west and give him peace. Then he had no doubt that he could eject Stanislaw and bring back and dominate Augustus. He knew that Stanislaw had close ties with France and he was willing at all costs to tie Moscow up with the coalition. He offered large sums of money to any nation that would help him. He offered to send 30,000 men to their assistance, even though he could ill spare them. He was willing to make peace on almost any terms, provided he could keep the small strip of the Neva which he had occupied and on which he was planning his new capital of St. Petersburg. He was willing to abandon Augustus, if he could only secure some prince to take the throne and successfully oppose Stanislaw and Charles. He offered it to the son of Sobieski, the same man whom Charles had selected. He offered it to Rakoczi of Transylvania and even to the Duke of Marlborough. More than that, he offered to make the latter Prince of Kiev, of Volodymyr or of Siberia—anything to secure aid against the victorious Swede. He added promises of wealth in jewels and lands. Still he found no takers.

On the other hand all this disturbed Mazeppa the more, for he realized from Peter's own actions that he intended to do away with the privileges of the Host. Such an offer was a direct violation of the articles that Mazeppa had signed on his "election" and which Peter had in effect ratified in 1689. He saw that the situation was more dangerous and more involved than did those officers who were so glibly asking why he did not call a halt to the aggression of Peter and support Stanislaw.

Peter's visit to Kiev in the summer of 1706 confirmed his suspicions. Menshikov, the former pastry-hawker, was uneducated and also the lover of Peter's second wife, Catherine, with Peter's knowledge and consent. Despite his humble origin or perhaps because of it, Menshikov was able and unscrupulous and constantly seeking for more power. He was still young, of Peter's generation and he enjoyed Peter's type of entertainment much better than he did Mazeppa's but the Hetman never showed any open signs of disapproval.

Sure of himself and of the friendship of Peter, Menshikov did not hesitate to express his feelings. At a banquet offered by Mazeppa in Kiev to the Tsar, Menshikov, decidedly intoxicated, came up to his host and remarked in an audible voice: "It is time to finish with our enemies." Mazeppa understood the allusion and calmly answered, "Not yet."

Menshikov looked at him with amazement: "The situation could not be more favorable, for the Tsar is here with his army."

The Hetman turned aside the comment: "It is dangerous to commence a second, internal war, without having finished the foreign foe."

Menshikov went on: "Must we then be afraid to wipe out the enemies of the Tsar? I do not believe it. Besides there is no one but you who is faithful to the Tsar. You must give another proof of your loyalty; you must make your memory eternal in the memory of the Russians. Future Tsars must be able to glorify your name and say that there was never but one Hetman who was absolutely loyal, Ivan Stepanovych Mazeppa, who performed the greatest service to the Russian state."

By now this obvious conversation was attracting the attention of the officers. Peter saw that his favorite had gone too far and he at once withdrew and with him the other Muscovites departed. Mazeppa was left alone with his officers, who had overheard the conversation. He quietly remarked:

"You have heard it; it is always the same story, at Moscow, here and everywhere. Lord, have mercy on us and do not let them carry out the plan they have conceived. Everywhere we are shedding our blood, in Livonia, Poland, Lithuania, the Crimea, among the Turks . . . And why? As our recompense we are insulted, humiliated, and now they ask us to sacrifice the last trace of our liberties."

He said no more but he allowed the officers to draw their own inferences.

Then another letter came from the Princess. She wrote that she had met in Lviv Boris Petrovich Sheremetev and General Renne in her guise as a supporter of Augustus. When she had praised the Hetman for his loyalty to the Tsar, Renne replied: "God have mercy upon the good and intelligent Mazeppa. The poor man does not know that Prince Alexander Danilovich Menshikov is digging a pit under him and wants himself to be the Hetman of Ukraine." When she begged them to warn Mazeppa, Renne and Sheremetev both refused on the ground that they did not dare.

Mazeppa had this letter read to his higher officers. Then he commented: "I know what they are preparing against me and all of us. They want to make me a Prince of the Holy Roman Empire; they want to suppress the chiefs of the Kozak state, annex our cities and send us their governors. If we resist their plans, they are thinking of driving us into Poland and filling our land with Muscovites. You heard at the last dinner the words of Menshikov. I know that he has asked from the Tsar the principality of Chernyhiv, a favor that he considers the first step toward the securing of the Hetmanate. I know also that feeling himself in danger, the Tsar has offered our Ukraine to an English lord, Marlborough. Our country is destined to be governed by a foreigner, a Muscovite or an Englishman. Lord, save us from the Russians."

The officers begged him to do something but he only turned to Orlyk: "Write Princess Dolska that I thank her for the valuable information which her friendship has sent me."

As a matter of fact Peter had arranged for Mazeppa to become a Prince of the Holy Roman Empire with his nephew Voynarovsky as his successor in the dignity. The Hetman had paid 3,000 ducats for it but he valued it more than he said to his officers. It might become an anchor to windward. The Hapsburgs were hostile to France. They were by no means consistently friendly to Poland. They were at the moment engaged in a dispute with Charles XII but if Mazeppa survived, he might as a Prince of the Holy Roman Empire again obtain the chance to pursue his own policy, if Peter and the Emperor happened to clash.

Whatever the role of Princess Dolska, she was not acting out of disinterested patriotism for Poland or love for Mazeppa. She charged and collected well for every piece of information which passed through her hands. One time the Hetman sent her 100,000 Carolinen in Czech money. Another time he casually left 10,000 ducats on one of her estates. Yet he had no doubt that she was one of his most trustworthy channels to the Polish court and might be able to secure him the access to Charles for which he was seeking.

It was more than a year since these strange negotiations began. So far they had been utterly fruitless, for Mazeppa was still waiting for some clue as to the intentions of the Swedish King. What did the King intend to do about Peter? But he had another problem no less serious. Could he trust his officers, when the moment for action came? Were their angry words so much talk which would vanish at the first touch of reality? Could he depend upon them or would some begin to intrigue against the Host for their own advantage?

CHAPTER FIFTEEN

THE DENUNCIATION BY KOCHUBEY

The year 1707 promised to drag on in the same futile negotiations and meaningless talk. Princess Dolska continued to write the most glowing promises in the name of King Stanislaw. Peter continued with his plans for turning the Kozak regiments into ordinary Russian troops and tried to find allies in the West. Charles still remained aloof in Saxony and received new reinforcements of men and supplies of ammunition. Mazeppa still sought in vain for a way out of his present situation without finding it.

In September, Augustus finally yielded. He signed the Treaty of Altranstädt, abdicated the Polish throne and promised to leave all anti-Swedish combinations. He also delivered up Patkul for execution. To do this, he had to slip away secretly from Peter's court.

The Tsar was furious and he at first thought of discarding Augustus entirely. Then he changed his mind and decided to keep him on the throne, whether he would or not. He found a section of the Polish magnates to help him. They formed a Confederation at Sandomierz and declared for Augustus. Nothing shows the Polish loss of morale so well as this. The magnates would not fight to keep Augustus on the throne but they were only too willing to obey Peter and acknowledge their loyalty to a man who had himself abandoned them. It underscored the untrustworthiness of Polish promises and confirmed the Hetman in his idea that he could make no move, until he heard from Charles himself.

Peter had won these magnates by promising them the control of the west bank of the Dnieper. He made it clear that Mazeppa was not going to succeed in bringing together under his control for Peter the two halves of Ukraine. The discrediting of Augustus had shown Peter that he could secure the whole of Poland and he had no desire at the moment to risk the alienation of Polish public opinion, whatever it was worth.

It is easy to appreciate Mazeppa's feelings. He had used all of his diplomatic skill in cementing his position on the west bank, even in the face of the opposition of Peter and Augustus but he realized that the time was coming when he would run out of excuses and be compelled to withdraw his regiments. Still he continued to hope. He kept finding more and more partisans of Charles and Stanislaw and week by week, month by month the withdrawal was postponed.

During the spring he made several visits to the headquarters of the Tsar. He could not fail to observe one thing. Peter still had full confidence in him but it was as Ivan Mazeppa, not as the Hetman of the Zaporozhian Host. The Tsar still believed that he was the only loyal Hetman that had held the post but the hour was coming when Mazeppa's reward for loyalty was to be his removal from his position and his inclusion in the Tsar's personal entourage.

Mazeppa was not satisfied. Wealth and rewards were not that for which he had been striving for thirty five years and more. He was proud of his position as the captain of the ship of Ukraine and he intended to continue in that position.

This came out very clearly at Zhovkva on April 11. Apparently at this meeting Peter told Mazeppa his future plans. The Hetman left, deeply shocked and found some excuse for not attending the banquet that night. The officers noticed Mazeppa's anxiety but he still said nothing and only remarked: "If I had served God as faithfully as I have the Tsar, I would have received the greatest of rewards. Here I can become an angel and my loyalty is not worth thanks."

It was again Menshikov who made clear the meaning of Mazeppa's words. The next day as Commander-in-Chief he began to issue orders to the Kozaks without consulting the Hetman. It was a sign that Peter was on the verge of executing his long cherished plans.

Mazeppa was desperate. He felt that at all costs he had to get in touch with the Swedish King. He renewed his relations with Princess Dolska and secretly left Zhovkva to meet her at one of her estates, even though he was supposed to be present in the suite of the Tsarevich Alexis. He tried other ways to approach Charles. He sent him an Orthodox monk and later a Bulgarian bishop whose name has not been preserved. All was without results. Charles was not going to commit himself until he was ready. Perhaps he did not yet know himself what he was going to do. Like most of the Europeans of his day he was very vague as to conditions within the domains of Peter. He had been away from Sweden for years and he had no access to the old records of the Swedish crown. It had been almost a half century since a Swedish King had conducted negotiations with a Ukrainian Hetman. Charles XII, like the other professional soldiers of the time, had little use for irregular cavalry. He thought in terms of the advanced military science. He still hoped that he could train a Polish army to assist him. King Stanislaw encouraged him in the idea, for he like all the other Poles still dreamed that he might be able to recover for the Republic the whole of Ukraine.

Finally the message came. On September 16, a Vlach peasant appeared with a letter from the Princess. For the first time in over a year the Hetman gave it to Orlyk to decipher but of course he repeated his protests at the machinations of the Princess. Her letter contained another from King Stanislaw. The King wrote that he was sending it on the same day that Charles had left Saxony for Poland. He added that he would carry out Mazeppa's wishes, as soon as the Swedish King approached the boundaries of Ukraine and he added the text of a proposed treaty in twelve articles.

The Hetman now realized that one thing was certain. If Charles were not going to turn east, he would not have returned to Poland. That meant he was going to attack Peter and the Hetman knew that if he did, his Kozaks would play a real part. Peter would not be able to risk an upheaval by abolishing the Host over night. It was for the Hetman to take advantage of this respite and secure something for his people.

For the first time he felt that he had to talk about his plans with someone and he chose the faithful Orlyk. To the latter's surprise, the next morning, the Hetman solved the mystery of the strange correspondence by swearing Orlyk to absolute secrecy and then saying that "for the sake of your wives and children, for the general good of my mother country Ukraine, the whole Zaporozhian Host and all the Little Russian people and for the advancement and spreading of the military rights and freedoms" he had opened negotiations with the enemy.

From this moment Orlyk became the right hand of the Hetman in the execution of his plans. He knew when Mazeppa sent the chaplain of Princess Dolska with a message to Charles, so that the King would realize the situation and not add to the woes of Ukraine by ravaging it with fire and sword.

It was just at this moment that Mazeppa became fully conscious of the dangers of his position. He had been thinking of taking more of the Officers' Council into his confidence but he was suddenly stopped. He learned that his old friend, Colonel Kochubey, had denounced his plans to Peter.

It had been nearly three years since the Hetman had approached Kochubey to ask for the hand of his daughter. The scandal had long since passed into history and Mazeppa had continued to treat his old friend with the greatest consideration. Kochubey and his wife had not forgotten. They were only waiting for an opportunity.

They found it when Mazeppa was absent from Baturyn and had placed Kochubey in command of the city. It gave the Colonel the opportunity and he took advantage of it to accuse the Hetman of intriguing with the Swedes and Poles.

He sent an Orthodox monk, one Nikanor, to carry his denunciation, including the Hetman's duma, to Moscow and he paid him for the trip. Then he sat back and waited. He apparently underestimated the Tsar's confidence in Mazeppa; he did not appreciate the fact that the Hetman had dissociated himself from the mur-

murings of the officers; he did not know or care what position a
new Hetman would have. He thought only of revenge.

Nikanor failed miserably. As soon as he delivered the message,
he was seized and taken to the torture chambers of Preobrazhenskoye. As soon as the torturers went to work on him, he broke
down and confessed that he had been hired by Kochubey and that
he knew nothing of the Hetman's movements except what he had
been told to say. Then he was thrown into prison, and kept
isolated, while the Tsar sent the story to the Hetman.

There was good reason for not believing Kochubey's story. The
Tsar and the court were fully confident of Mazeppa's loyalty. They
were not so sure of the officers. They knew of the opposition of
the men around the Hetman and they were convinced that they
would stop at nothing to discredit Mazeppa for his loyalty to Peter.
Such conduct had long been common. Their mistake was that
they assumed that Kochubey was in this conspiracy and did not
dream that he was actuated only by his desire for revenge.

Kochubey was disturbed because his messenger did not return
but he still did not take any precautions. He was sure that he was
right and after a few months, he decided to try again. He sent a
man by the name of Yatsenenko to the Tsar's chaplain and he
added more details to his earlier story. Among these was the true
fact that the Hetman had seen a Jesuit, Father Zelenski, who was
in the Jesuit College in Vinnytsya and was an agent of King
Stanislaw. Then to add a touch of melodrama he told the fantastic
story that Mazeppa was plotting against Peter's life and had posted
three hundred serdyuks, his professional solders, to shoot the Tsar,
when Peter had been thinking of visiting Baturyn. This detail
was enough to discredit the entire story. Yatsenenko in turn
disappeared.

Still Kochubey did not realize what was going on. He met his
friend Colonel Iskra of the Poltava Regiment at Dikanka, later
the scene of Gogol's celebrated stories, and the two men worked
out the details of the plot. They elaborated the stories and sent a
priest named Svyataylo to convey their tale to the Colonel of one

of the Muscovite regiments. They hoped in this way to bypass any channels where Mazeppa might have influence and so reach higher circles in Moscow.

It was now the spring of 1708 and Mazeppa was fully conscious of the danger around him. True to his system of taking the initiative against attack, he reported himself to Peter the denunciation of Kochubey and Iskra and he asked the Tsar to investigate the charges against himself. Peter was completely disarmed by this apparent frankness and on March 1 and again on the 11, he twice assured the Hetman of his confidence. The two men talked over the situation and Peter advised the Hetman to remove the danger by arresting the unruly colonels who were grumbling against the Muscovite authorities, especially Colonel Danylo Apostol of Mirhorod. Peter gave Kochubey the credit for more intelligence than he possessed and was sure that he was merely the agent of a conspiracy that desired to get the Hetman out of the way so as to join the Swedes, once he was gone.

Mazeppa had his own ideas and he tried to arrest Kochubey and Iskra but they escaped his troops and took refuge with the Muscovites. While they were there, Peter's Chancellor Golovkin with the characteristic duplicity of the times sent them a cordial invitation to visit the capital and report on the misdeeds of Mazeppa and on April 18, Kochubey, Iskra, Yatsenenko (who had reappeared), Svyataylo, Captain Kovanko, two secretaries, a nephew of Colonel Iskra and eight servants reached the Russian capital.

They were overjoyed at their reception. The Chancellor and Baron Shafirov, one of Peter's most accomplished diplomats, met them and assured them of the Tsar's interest and gratitude. They were royally entertained and flattered and were encouraged to tell all they knew.

Kochubey, a tiresome speaker, droned out an apparently endless list of the sins of Mazeppa and the other colonels. There was nothing too small to be mentioned and there was hardly a detail that was not already known through Mazeppa by the Muscovite agents. Here are a few of the charges:

1. At Minsk in 1706, Mazeppa had privately remarked to Kochubey that he had received a letter from King Stanislaw through Princess Dolska and that the King had promised to make him Prince of Chernyhiv and to give liberty to the Zaporozhian Host. (Incidentally Mazeppa had forwarded this letter to Peter and the title mentioned was the one that Menshikov wanted.)

2. On May 11, 1707, Mazeppa had toasted Princess Dolska and declared that she was a noble and intelligent woman and his friend. (Everyone knew this, including Sheremetev and Renne.)

3. The same year when Mazeppa had been with Kochubey and his daughter at the baptism of some Jew, he had remarked that Moscow wished to enslave Ukraine. (This was the common talk of the entire Host, officers and men.)

4. On September 20, 1707, the Jesuit Zelenski had visited Mazeppa and in a talk to the colonels had advised them not to fear the Swedes, for they were intending to fight Moscow and not the Kozaks. (It was impossible to keep out of the army Poles and Roman Catholics, while the army was holding the west bank in an ostensible desire to satisfy the Poles and maintain their sovereignty.)

5. On October 8, after a ball at Kiev, at which the Colonels of Mirhorod and Pryluky were present, Mazeppa had sent a Kozak to the same Zelenski. Of course this was treasonable, for the Hetman should not have personal contact with a Jesuit. (How could Mazeppa in his position in Poland help it?)

6. On October 10, Mazeppa had read to the Colonels the text of the Treaty of Hadyach, drawn up by Vyhovsky fifty years before. (This was a well-known document.)

7. At Christmas Mazeppa had met secretly and at night the same Zelenski.

8. The Hetman had threatened to execute his opponents. (Who were they?)

9. At the house of Kochubey, Mazeppa had seemed sad and said: "What is the consolation that I have in living in constant

danger? Am I not the bull that is waiting to be butchered at any moment?" He had then praised Vyhovsky and Bryukhovetsky, two Hetmans who had opposed Moscow and had remarked to Madame Kochubey: "I would have thought of our liberty but no one wants to help me, and your husband least of all."

10. One day at Kiev Mazeppa had told the colonels that he was not planning to make his nephew Voynarovsky Hetman in his place, for he could live without that. Then he added: "If there is any one here who can save the country, I will leave it in his charge. But if you keep this burden on my shoulders, listen to me and follow me."

11. The Hetman was doing his best to prevent marriages between Muscovites and Ukrainians.

12. When some one complained of the Tatars, Mazeppa remarked: "Let them alone. They will be useful to us."

With the exception of Point 9, there was little or nothing important or significant. Kochubey had shown a surprising knowledge of the meetings of Mazeppa and Zelenski as well as of Princess Dolska, but Peter already had most of this information with Mazeppa's own explanations. The authorities wanted to know what went on at these meetings but Kochubey could not enlighten them, except by drawing upon his imagination and this took such fantastic forms that he was obviously making his stories up and not giving real facts.

Mazeppa had not trusted only to verbal arguments in his defence. At the news of Kochubey's denunciation, he had begun with infinite tact to give valuable presents to every one who would be connected with the investigation. He gave Peter 2,000 ducats, Menshikov 1000 and six large silver bottles, Golovkin 1000, Sheremetev 500 and some silver dishes, Shafirov 500, Dolgoruky 600 and Stefanov 100 ducats. This was nothing unusual, for the Hetman was known for his liberality but once more it turned the entire court in his favor. The investigators decided to go over carefully the stories told by Kochubey.

They soon found inconsistencies between the tales of Kochubey and Iskra, when they were examined separately. So they finally decided to put Iskra to the torture. They had hardly started, when he broke down and made the crucial admission: "I know nothing of the treason of Mazeppa except what Kochubey told me."

By this time the Muscovites had become convinced that Kochubey was the ringleader and perhaps the sole instigator of the conspiracy. They concentrated their attention upon him and increased the tortures applied. Even before they started, Kochubey lost his courage and confessed:

"I confess that I invented this story because of my hate for Mazeppa for the insult that he gave my house."

Now the real truth was out but the investigators, desirous of linking Kochubey with the conspiracy among the officers, refused to believe it. They were sure that Kochubey was also in the pro-Swedish and anti-Muscovite conspiracy. So they gave him five blows with the knout and kept repeating:

"Did you not make up this story in the interest of the Swedes, so as to have a loyal Hetman deposed and replace him with a man who would be open to the suggestions of our enemies?"

Kochubey denied it but no one believed him.

On April 30, the investigators sent Kochubey, Iskra and their party to the Tsar at Smolensk with the recommendation that Kochubey and Iskra be put to death and that the others be deported to Siberia.

Peter was not satisfied. He was still certain that there was a widespread conspiracy among the Kozak officers and with the increasing menace of Charles who was by now attacking with his main army, he wanted assurance doubly sure that there was no treason in his ranks and he called for still sterner measures and more cruel tortures. It was in vain that Golovkin and Shafirov argued that Kochubey might not live to be executed, if it were done. Peter was inexorable and the tortures went on.

The prisoners were taken to Vitebsk where they again received the attention of the Muscovites. Kochubey received five blows of the knout, Iskra six, Father Svyataylo 20 and Captain Kovanko 14. Of course nothing more was discovered. Kochubey and Iskra had not been in the movement of the officers and they could add nothing to their previous stories.

Captain Kovanko furnished a touch of grim humor to the miserable scene. He cried out under the flogging, "The knout is so agreeable that it ought to be given as a present to women." It was perfectly evident that he was thinking of Madame Kochubey who had been the cause of the whole attack on Mazeppa.

The tortures went on and finally when the ringleaders were utterly broken, the Tsar sent them back to the Hetman for final judgment. They reached his headquarters at Borshchahovka near Bila Tserkva on July 11. Mazeppa had been thoroughly cleared and the attempt to take vengeance on him for his relations with Motrya had recoiled upon the own heads of his accusers.

Mazeppa had it in his power to spare them but he decided against it. He was perfectly conscious that he was engaged in the dangerous task of moving against Peter and Kochubey had come too close for comfort in his estimation of the Hetman's motives. He was afraid that any pardon might reflect some personal hesitation and start new suspicions against him.

In addition to this, he had good reason to be angry at Kochubey. The colonel had insulted him in his deepest feelings through his treatment of Motrya. The Hetman had proposed to her in good faith. She had been the one object of his real affection and her loss had made him feel his loneliness more than ever. Both as political and military leader and as lover he had suffered from Kochubey and he determined that the two ringleaders should die.

Three days later, the entire Kozak army was drawn up in a hollow square. Kochubey and Iskra were brought in. A recorder read the sentence and a priest appeared to give the last consolation to their souls. Then the two men knelt down and laid their heads upon the blocks. The axes of the executioners flashed in the sunlight and in a moment the two heads were rolling on the ground.

The hushed and solemn crowds dispersed. The troops left the place of execution and Mazeppa, freed from this last threat, remained with his own thoughts, his vengeance achieved and the confidence that Peter had in him still unshaken.

It had been a narrow escape, more perhaps by good fortune than by wise planning. It made him resolve to be still more cautious, still more secretive until the decisive moment came.

CHAPTER SIXTEEN

THE SECRET ALLIANCE

In September, 1707, Charles XII reached Warsaw to make his final preparations for his attack on Peter. His goal was clear. He intended to seize and occupy Moscow and to depose Peter as he had Augustus. What were his direct plans and how was he going to implement them?

This was the question that bothered Ivan Mazeppa, as he redoubled his efforts to come to a definite understanding with the Swedish King before he threw off the mask of loyalty to Peter. It was not an easy question for Charles kept his own counsel and neither Stanislaw, Dolska or Peter had the slightest hint of his thoughts, as he waited for reinforcements to arrange for the decisive blow.

There were three routes open to him. The first was in the north. In one sense it was the most advantageous for Charles, for his garrisons in Finland protected his left flank. These under General Lebeker could support him much of the way. Unfortunately during the course of the war, Peter had recaptured Narva and had secured a foothold on the Neva River and had built on it a fort, the nucleus of the future St. Petersburg. Peter had devastated the country in this area and it would be difficult for Charles to supply his army on this route.

Mazeppa was glad of this. If Charles had taken the northern route, the Swedish forces would have been nowhere near Ukraine. The Kozaks would have been left without any support and Peter would have had a good chance of calling the Kozak regiments to his assistance and moving them from Ukraine before the Hetman was finally ready. In addition to that, a complete victory would merely strengthen the Poles and make Charles less amenable to the requests and needs of the Kozaks.

159

The second route was in the south through Ukraine. This had the advantage of allowing the King to move through unravaged territory and of crossing into Muscovite territory when he wished. Its disadvantage was equally obvious. Ukraine would become the battleground of the armies. Mazeppa had been at too many of Peter's councils of war not to know that he intended to devastate the land through which Charles was going to march and unless the Kozaks could take the initiative and expel all the Muscovite forces, the results for Ukraine and the Ukrainian people would be disastrous and the horrors of the old Ruin would be repeated on an even greater scale.

The third route was in the centre through Smolensk. It would bring Charles near enough to Ukraine to offer him support and yet give a more or less free hand to the Host. Its value to the Kozaks would depend upon the actions of the Poles. If they rallied to the cause of Stanislaw and mobilized a strong army, they might reap the major fruits of victory. Mazeppa did not believe they would. He was too familiar with Polish politics and Polish factionalism to worry about a Polish regeneration at the crucial moment.

The decisive moment was approaching and it would not be long before the fortune of Ukraine would be decided. The Hetman would become the ruler of an independent state or Ukraine might be incorporated with Swedish permission into a common state with Poland or Peter would win the struggle and absorb it into his reorganized Russian Empire. The burden was on the shoulders of Mazeppa himself. The strain was becoming terrible and almost unbearable and the denunciation by Kochubey and the knowledge that there were other officers who sided with him added to the anxieties of the aged Hetman. He felt it necessary to redouble his efforts at secrecy. His long years of experience had made caution his second nature and he was able to carry on the necessary diplomatic conversations without arousing the suspicions of the Tsar or the Muscovites in his capital of Baturyn.

Yet there was one other quality needed. That was daring and a willingness to run calculated risks. There would come a moment when the Hetman had to decide upon immediate and swift action. He would have to throw off the mask or see his plans miscarry through his failure to do so. If he declared himself too soon, he would lose but if he missed the golden moment, it would never return. Here was Mazeppa's weakness. He could be resolute and determined but old age and the habits of years had dimmed his capacity for taking risks. He wanted to be sure of his ground before he acted and there was much to do.

The result was the unreal and even fantastic events of the first half of 1708. Disguised messengers, Roman Catholic monks and Orthodox clergy wandered back and forth, until it seemed again as if all the participants were engaged in some unreal play and not in a struggle for life or death. Mazeppa was still not satisfied. He wanted a perfect combination but it did not seem to come.

He had also deep personal trouble. His mother, the aged Abbess Mary Magdalen, was dying in Kiev in her convent. She was well over ninety before her health finally broke and then she lingered on helpless for months. The Hetman stayed as much as possible in Kiev with her and her illness offered him a good excuse for not making up his mind. He did not fail to keep both Peter and Menshikov fully informed, as her condition became more and more hopeless. Finally in November 1707, she passed away and he returned to Baturyn.

Her death left an unfillable gap in his life. It would be an exaggeration to say that she had dominated him, but he admitted frankly to Peter, to Menshikov, to Orlyk and to all his friends that he had always followed her advice. It was her influence that had kept him from making mistakes in his early years. More than once her influence in powerful quarters in Moscow had extricated him from difficulties which he had created or into which he had fallen. She had been his one confidante, his one political guide, and now at the most critical moment of his career, he was deprived of her calm and practical advice. He had only Orlyk with him and Orlyk was still relatively untried and without any experience except what the Hetman had given him.

Charles spent the autumn in Warsaw. The Polish magnates who supported Stanislaw wined and dined Charles and danced to his success. They were only too happy to see him move against their own enemy Peter but they had made it clear that they were not interested in raising an army to assist him. Throughout the entire contest, the Poles had done their best to remain neutral, while Muscovites, Kozaks, Saxons and Swedes had moved across their soil, pillaging as they went. Their participation was confined to personal and family feuds. This was a disappointment to Charles who was a warrior before everything else and it inclined him, despite any prejudices, to pay steadily increasing attention to the role of the Kozaks.

Another point that was brought more and more to his attention was the role of the southern neighbors of Poland and Ukraine. All the European ambassadors at the court of the Sultan appreciated the anxiety of the Turks at the steady advance of Peter to the south and his hopes for securing control over the Tatars of the Crimea. They reported this to their home governments and Charles noted with some surprise that both the French and their enemies in the War of the Spanish Succession were agreed that Charles, whatever his next move, would do well to seek for allies among the Mohammedan countries. King Stanislaw stressed the same idea and it was not long before Mohammedan diplomatic agents began to appear at Charles' headquarters.

All this gradually aroused in the mind of the Swedish King an appreciation of the significance of Mazeppa and the Kozaks. In the beginning he had thought of connections only with Poland and its aspirations. He heard incessantly that the Kozaks wanted to form part of the Polish Republic and it was through Polish channels that he had received the first overtures from Mazeppa. Now he was being reoriented and as the promised armies of Stanislaw failed to appear, he was compelled to look elsewhere for allies, even though he was still sceptical of the value of troops that were not trained along European lines.

This explains many of the peculiarities of the policy of the Swedish King. It is still a disputed point in military history whether Charles took the wisest course in leaving Warsaw for Wilno and attempting to push his way to the east from northern Poland and Lithuania. At the same time he sent General Krassau with a Swedish corps and the Polish army toward Kiev, while he led his Swedish troops to Grodno and Smolensk.

Mazeppa did not like this movement of the Poles toward Ukraine, for he knew how unpopular the Poles were in these regions. Its only good point was that it gave him a good excuse for concentrating his forces to meet the new menace and thus it brought his troops, some 40,000 men, together.

Charles had some 35,000 Swedes with him at the start of the campaign. He left 8,000 in Poland. In addition to this, General Loewenhaupt had 11,000 in Livonia and General Lebeker 15,000 in Finland. He had thus in the various sectors almost 68,000 trained men and the really trained forces of Peter were scarcely more numerous, although they had the advantage of moving on the inner line and were able to ravage and devastate the country through which Charles had to march.

It is difficult to know whether Charles was really planning to break through at Smolensk. He made superhuman efforts during the winter but with the spring of 1708 he definitely began to swing toward the south. Everywhere Peter kept opposite to him and it seemed impossible for the Swedes to find an area which Peter had not laid waste.

At the same time the Tsar endeavored to strengthen the hold of the Poles over the area west of the Dnieper. He kept ordering Mazeppa to withdraw and to transfer to the command of the Grand Marshal Sieniawski some 10,000 Kozaks. Sieniawski was Peter's latest choice for prominence in Poland. Again this transfer of Kozaks to Polish command was counter to the interests of Mazeppa and he continued to avoid compliance.

He found a good excuse. Sieniawski was an insignificant man but his wife Elizabeth, Palatine of Belz, was a very able and successful dabbler in Polish politics. She had succeeded in securing contacts with both Charles and Mazeppa and kept him informed of her husband's plans. She inclined herself to the cause of King Stanislaw. Mazeppa used this very effectively with the Tsar. He argued with a great deal of plausibility that she was leading Sieniawski to play the Swedish game and that the detachment of his Kozaks would prove a boomerang. With more truth he explained that the Kozaks would not fight ardently under Polish command.

He won his fight temporarily but as Charles swung toward the Dnieper after defeating the Russians at Holovchyn in July, Peter knew that Charles would renew the pressure. He was constantly urging the Hetman to detach troops for service in the various armies. Bulavin had been defeated in the east but Peter insisted on detaching various regiments and even talked of ordering the entire Kozak army to leave Ukraine and join General Infland in the north. Each new command increased the murmuring of the officers. This reached the ears of the Tsar and made him still more eager to break up the compact mass of Mazeppa's forces, lest they actually revolt against their Hetman.

Then Mazeppa was taken ill with the gout and during the winter of 1707-1708 and the spring of 1708, he was confined to his bed, seemingly unable to handle the affairs of the Host. How far this was a feigned illness cannot be determined. He was carrying a terrific burden and was under a terrible strain in simultaneously negotiating with Charles and in thwarting the demands of Peter. Besides he was not a young man and his mother's death had greatly affected him, while the intrigues of Kochubey made him still more suspicious. Peter sent him his own physician but he was unable to help the Hetman and the Tsar saw with profound regret that Mazeppa was apparently losing control of the situation. The Hetman was not sorry to give this impression to a certain degree but it was risky, for Peter might jump to the conclusion that he was finished, remove him from his position and with expressions of sympathy and honors to his old friend, either appoint a Hetman out of the more pro-Muscovite officers or even abolish the post.

All this time Mazeppa was stocking Baturyn and other cities with arms and foodstuffs. He did it openly on the excuse that if Charles did invade Ukraine, these fortified cities could hold up his advance until Peter's forces were able to come to their rescue.

Sometime during the spring Colonels Apostol of Mirhorod, Horlenko of Pryluky and Selenko of Lubny and the artillery commander Lomykovsky, the leaders of the more outspoken officers, demanded of Mazeppa that he try to get in touch with Charles, before it was too late. Mazeppa finally took with them an oath that he would do so when Charles approached Ukraine, but he gave them no hint that the negotiations were already under way.

However some time in the spring, perhaps when Charles was at Smorhony in February, the negotiations took a serious turn and some sort of an understanding was reached. Later Orlyk gave the text of this treaty or at least extracts from it. They were as follows:

Article I. His Royal Majesty promises to defend Ukraine and the part of the territory of the Kozaks which is annexed to it and to send without any delay supporting troops when necessity demands it or the Hetman and the Estates request it. These troops on their entrance will remain under the orders of the Swedish commanders, but while they are there employed, His Majesty will entrust the direction to the Prince or his successors who will maintain it as long as they have need of the troops. His Royal Majesty will furnish their pay and the Kozaks their bread and food.

Article II. All that is conquered of the old possession of Moscow will belong by right of conquest to him who makes himself master; but whatever is discovered as having belonged to the old Ruthenian people will be returned or kept for the principality of Ukraine.

Article III. The Prince and the Estates of Ukraine will be kept and maintained by virtue of the law which they have hitherto enjoyed throughout the Principality and the parts annexed to it.

Article IV. Ivan Mazeppa, legitimate Prince of Ukraine, will not be disturbed in any manner in the possession of this principality. After his death (and it is hoped that this may be long postponed), liberty will be preserved for the Estates of Ukraine in accordance with their rights and ancient laws.

Article V. No change shall be introduced in the present usage in regard to the arms and title of the Prince of Ukraine. His Royal Majesty will never assume this title or these arms.

Article VI. For greater security and in accordance with this treaty, the Prince and the Estates will hand over to His Royal Majesty for the duration of the war and the emergency some of the cities, i.e. Starodub, Mhlyn, Poltava, Baturyn and Hadyach.

This Treaty agrees in full detail with the later policy of Orlyk after Mazeppa's death. It makes no reference to King Stanislaw or the Poles. On the other hand an anonymous Swedish account in describing a somewhat similar treaty states that it was concluded between Charles, Stanislaw and Mazeppa and is rather vague as to whether Poland and Ukraine were to have some organic relation or not. It is perhaps possible that there was some written understanding between all parties without the conclusion of a formal treaty which would be difficult to arrange and sign in view of the secrecy with which negotiations were being carried on. We cannot be sure even of the definite text for all the records and other papers of Charles were later destroyed as were the archives of the Hetman and this leaves the details of the actual course of events very vague and dependent upon the memory of Orlyk and some of the associates of Charles.

At all events only Orlyk and Voynarovsky seem to have been kept informed as to the actual state of the negotiations, which were still unknown even to Mazeppa's closest friends among the officers.

At this point Mazeppa's habitual caution began to be a handicap; yet with the affair of Kochubey still going on, it is hard to see how the old Hetman could have ventured to prepare the officers and still less the men and the population for the coming events. He and they were surrounded by the secret agents of the Tsar who already suspected the officers of what they were really planning and it was only the Hetman personally who had completely covered his tracks.

Mazeppa displayed the most ostentatious joy at all the victories of the Muscovites. He had services in all the Churches on the occasion of each victory or near victory. He congratulated Peter on all possible occasions. He sent money to Menshikov to buy him a palace in Moscow, so that he could be more frequently in the Russian capital and be less burdensome there to his friends. Not a word or sign did he reveal of what he was really planning.

This was all to the good, for Charles was steadily approaching the borders of Ukraine and would soon be able to help him. Yet this increased his danger and his difficulties. He had determined to wait until Charles crossed the border. With each advance of the Swedes, Peter redoubled his efforts. When Mazeppa continued to report the discontent of the officers, Peter sent troops into Ukraine to support the Hetman in putting down the revolts and Mazeppa was unable to reject the proffered aid, although he wanted to get as many of the Muscovites as possible out of Ukraine.

The reverses of some of the generals of Charles, slight as they were at the period, cast a damper on the spirits of the officers and the population. They began to doubt the possibility of a Swedish victory. The more ardent officers tended to become lukewarm as they saw the Hetman going out of his way to be ostentatiously loyal and some of them began to wonder whether they had not been mistaken in assuming that Mazeppa even slightly sympathized with them in their difficulties with the Muscovites.

Thus life went on at Baturyn throughout the summer. The strange messengers kept coming and going with ever greater frequency but not a hint was given as to their purpose. Mazeppa seemed oblivious to everything. Only Orlyk and Voynarovsky were aware of what was happening. The others felt that they were drifting into an impossible position, that they were being abandoned or falling between the policies of Peter and Charles. They needed encouragement and they did not receive it. Mazeppa seemed unable to move. He was still the captain of the ship but was he willing to give the orders, as the ship was drifting upon the rocks? No one seemed to know and the Hetman did not commit himself.

CHAPTER SEVENTEEN

THE MEETING OF CHARLES AND MAZEPPA

On September 16, 1708, Charles and his army entered Ukraine. It was already too late in the season for decisive operations before the winter commenced. The King had spent the greater part of the summer near the fortress of Mohyliv, trying to find a way to turn the Russian lines and approach Moscow from the direction of Kaluga. It was in vain for Peter kept his forces facing the Swedish King, constantly withdrawing and devastating the country which he had abandoned.

Now in the early autumn Charles gave up these futile manoeuvres and turned south. His army was delighted with Ukraine. For the first time in months, it had entered a region which had not been laid waste, a region offering an abundance of food and shelter and they looked forward to spending the winter there and resuming the campaign in the spring.

As in the case of so many of the movements of Charles XII, it is easier to trace the course of events than to fathom the reasons for them. Exactly why did Charles enter Ukraine? Did he do so at some request of Mazeppa or did he initiate the move in a moment of discouragement? The answer is not easy for Charles took no one into his confidence and apparently Mazeppa himself was surprised by this move.

Charles possibly made it on the spur of the moment to rest his tired soldiers and to secure additional supplies. He possibly did it to try out the promises of Mazeppa, now that he had been discouraged by the impossibility of securing effective aid from Poland. It is not impossible that he had already been converted to the idea of a great alliance of Sweden, Ukraine, Poland, Turkey and the Crimea against Moscow and that he wished to be in a favorable position for exploiting and developing this.

Yet there he was and Mazeppa's actions are no less difficult to explain. He had won his long diplomatic campaign to secure full recognition of his position and that of the Kozaks from Charles. He had a treaty or agreement of alliance and had promised to move when Charles entered Ukraine. Yet he did nothing. Perhaps he was waiting for Charles to come nearer to Baturyn and hoping that the King would move along the northern border of the country, so as to spare Ukraine the risk of devastation by Peter.

Even when he learned that Charles was already in Ukraine, he openly regretted the movement. To his officers he simply declared: "It is the devil who sends him here. He is going to ruin all my plans and bring to us in his wake the Russian forces. Now our Ukraine is devastated and lost." A surprising statement from a man who had been working for years to bring about an alliance with the Swedes.

For the moment he had his troops in hand but Peter was insisting with ever more vehemence that units be detached to cooperate with General Infland in the neighborhood of Starodub. Mazeppa's apparent hesitation proved disastrous in several regions.

It had been arranged that Charles would move to Starodub and occupy that important fortress. The Colonel in command was one of the most anti-Muscovite Ukrainian officers and believed that the Kozaks should join the Swedes. By an accident General Lagerkrone with his forces lost his way as he was approaching and passed some distance from the city. This gave General Infland commanding the Muscovite troops an opportunity to reach Starodub first. The Kozaks, had they known that Lagerkrone was approaching, could have held out until the arrival of the Swedish force. The Colonel had received no message from Mazeppa and the surprised officer saw himself forced to admit Infland. That cost the Hetman one of his important regiments and also one of his bases.

At the same time Charles met with another catastrophe. He had ordered General Loewenhaupt to bring him most of the 11,000 men and the munition supplies in Livonia. The sudden entrance of Charles into Ukraine compelled Loewenhaupt to change his line of march and he was attacked and defeated by the Muscovite armies under the command of Peter himself at the battle of Lesnaya on October 10. They captured or destroyed the entire convoy of Loewenhaupt. He escaped himself and joined Charles with some 6,000 discouraged and defeated soldiers. This meant that Charles could not hope soon for reinforcements and supplies from Sweden and that he was obliged to risk the fate of the campaign on the forces that he had with him and the troops of Mazeppa.

While all this was happening, the Hetman sent Charles a mission composed of a Kozak named Bystrytsky and a Livonian who had entered the service of the Hetman, perhaps as a representative of Charles. Bystrytsky carried no letters but a verbal message urging the King to seize the town of Novhorod Siversky ahead of the Muscovites. From there it would be easy for the King to reach the River Desna where Mazeppa would meet him.

Again misfortune dogged the plan. Charles only lost a few hours in starting but that was sufficient to allow the cavalry of Menshikov to reach and enter the city. Again it was as at Starodub. The commander of the Kozak garrison had no orders to admit the Swedish King and once more Menshikov was able to reap the profit. Yet it is remarkable that Charles made no reproach to the Hetman because of his dilatory tactics and his failure to notify his subordinates.

Mazeppa's lethargy seemed to increase with the passing weeks. His health deteriorated. His gout confined him to his bed and it always became worse when representatives of the Tsar visited Baturyn. Perhaps it was the result of the nervous strain under which he was laboring. Perhaps he was unable to rouse his aged mind and body to take the definite step of throwing off that allegiance which he had maintained so many years. Perhaps it was the loss by death of all those persons to whom he would have liked to show a free Ukraine. Mazeppa continued to do nothing and the few men who were the centre of the movement began to despair.

At the end of September, the Hetman called a meeting at Baturyn of his most trusted officers. They included Lomykovsky and a

few others. There was a frank discussion and the Hetman was
as non-committal as ever. Finally Colonel Lomykovsky spoke up
for the group:

"Without the Swedes, what can Ukraine and the Zaporozhian
Host hope for? What have you made your preparations for?"

Mazeppa flared back: "What good is it to tell you things in
advance? Trust my conscience and my modest brain; they will not
lose you. Thank God. I have as much sense as you."

Other officers seconded Lomykovsky without a dissenting voice.
Mazeppa remained impassive, the same elegant, aged figure. Suddenly he turned, left his place, walked over to a secret hiding place
in the wall and took out a paper. Orlyk read the terms of the alliance with Charles XII. Not one of the men had dreamed that
the Hetman had already done the very thing that they were urging
him to do. It was the first real information that the inner group
of his officers had that something was really under way.

There was no one to betray the Hetman but chance almost did.
A few days later a Pole carrying a message from Charles to Mazeppa
fell into the hands of the Muscovites. It was an appeal to the Hetman to join him with his troops. The Russians could scarcely believe their eyes and though the letter went to the highest authorities, it was forwarded to Mazeppa for his comments. No one believed that the Hetman was himself involved but it served to put
more pressure upon him to send part of his troops to the Muscovite
army.

Still Mazeppa continued the same policy. Now and then he was
forced to detach a few men. When the Tsar summoned him, he
pleaded that his health was too bad for him to issue the necessary
orders. Now he made the pretext that disloyalty and treason were
so rife that he did not dare to move them and that he would
need Muscovite aid to maintain order, if he let his own regiments
move. Peter was only too willing to oblige him and send his own
forces into Ukraine, so that Mazeppa's plan finally worked against
himself. Peter became more and more peremptory in his tone.
Menshikov crossed the River Snov and demanded that Mazeppa join

him. Again on October 31, he promised to do so even if it caused his death. When an envoy arrived to acknowledge this message he found the Hetman in bed, receiving the last rites of the Church. He reported to Peter that Mazeppa was really dying and advised him to take thought as to who was to be appointed to succeed him. At the same time in response to the renewed demands, Mazeppa sent his nephew Voynarovsky on October 22 to Menshikov's headquarters to protest at the renewed orders to devastate the country in advance of Charles.

The hours of possible hesitation were running out. Scarcely had the Russian representative left, when Mazeppa dashed off a note to Count Piper, the Chancellor of Charles, to arrange for contact between the Polish and Ukrainian armies. He also sent Bystrytsky back to the King to arrange for a meeting on the Desna on November 2, near the town of Makeshyn on the Desna. November 2 came and went without any activity.

Late in the afternoon of November 3, Mazeppa and his higher officers were at his chateau at Borzna, not far from Baturyn. They had had an elaborate dinner, as always when the Hetman was present and after the dinner, they were sitting around, indulging in their usual merriment and the light conversation which Mazeppa loved. The old man was still as non-committal as ever. In fact he was avoiding serious discussion.

Suddenly the officers heard the sound of galloping hoofs— some couriers probably, but the horses seemed almost exhausted from the sound, although they were being pushed to top speed. It seemed strange but stranger yet was the figure that stumbled into the room. It was Voynarovsky who had been half hostage and half guest at the headquarters of Menshikov. He was not that neat and elegantly dressed figure whom they all knew. He was exhausted, disheveled and dust-covered after a hard ride.

He did not wait for the usual formalities of the Hetman's court but as soon as he caught sight of his uncle, he blurted out the message he had come to deliver. "Menshikov will be here tomorrow, he is following me . . . my horses are better than his. I escaped secretly, when I heard one German officer say to another in his own language, 'Yes, may the Lord protect the Kozaks, for tomorrow they will be in irons.' " The end had come for the Host. Menshikov and Peter had made up their minds. They were so sure that Mazeppa was dying that they had decided to wait no longer.

At this staggering news, the officers present jumped up, drew their swords and surrounded the Hetman as if to protect him from an onrushing foe. The aged Hetman sat still.

Suddenly as if by magic the years rolled away and he leaped to his feet. He was no longer the aged and infirm figure whose death Peter had been awaiting. He was the fiery Kozak, every inch a leader of men. At his commanding gesture, the officers sheathed their swords. Then rang out the one order:

"Mount and ride for Baturyn."

It was the work of moments for the horses to be saddled, a column was formed and with Mazeppa at the head, it started.

That November night looked down on a wild ride. The peasants along the road were startled as they saw the Hetman leading his men at breakneck speed. It had been twenty years since Mazeppa rode as he did that night along the Baturyn road. It was not the solemn and dignified procession of a figure majestic and aloof. It was the wild rush of the traditional Kozak charge and it was headed by a Kozak Hetman of the old type, the man who dared to lead where others dared not follow.

The years had dropped away. Gone was the pose of indifference, the theatrical emphasis on detail and on formality. Mazeppa was free at last, free to say what he thought, to do as he thought best, and he was riding with the fate of Ukraine and the Host driving him on.

For a moment the past flashed through his mind, the years of flattery and of service, the years when his opinion was that of Jan Kazimierz, of Doroshenko, Samoylovych, Golitsyn and Peter. Now he was his own master, for he could shape his own policy for the good of Ukraine. He was returning to Baturyn the Hetman of Ukraine, an independent sovereign of an independent state. He was going to the camp of Charles not as a vassal but as the head of the Zaporozhian Host and the ruler of Ukraine. There was no need or time to dwell upon the past. He was living in the future.

For decades he had lived for this moment, he had planned for it. Now in his old age that moment for which he had dreamed had come and he had to check and recheck the orders that he had to give.

The startled warders at Baturyn saw the group gallop in. It was late but there was no sleep that night at Baturyn. There was too much to do.

The first thing was to get rid of the Muscovites. Mazeppa roused Colonel Annenkov, the Tsar's resident and spy, and sent him off in state with a letter to Menshikov, apologizing for the rudeness of Voynarovsky, an excitable young man who had forgotten his manners and left without saying the proper farewells. The agent grumbled and wondered but he had to go and off he went.

Then the orders rang out. Orlyk was sent to pack the most important documents in the archives to accompany Mazeppa and to burn the rest. That done, he allowed the Secretary to select some of the finest volumes in the library to take with him. The regimental officers were ordered to have their men ready at dawn "to meet the Swedes." Mazeppa did not explain. Those who were pro-Muscovite thought that the Hetman had recovered his senses. The patriots wondered whether the Hetman was going to fight the Swedes or what. They could not tell but one and all obeyed. Still other men of high rank received commands to fetch from the treasury barrels of coins. It seemed a strange order for the start of a campaign but no one asked a question. Something had happened. They had been accustomed to obey the Hetman before but there was no disobeying or hesitating before the crisp and vigorous orders of Mazeppa now.

There was nothing for him to do himself but he had no thought of sleeping. He wandered through the spacious halls of his palace. He had built it in the hope that it would be a worthy residence for a free Hetman. It was not built to house a slave of Peter. He thought of the figures in his past, of his mother who had not

lived until this hour; he thought of Motrya Kochubey and her dis-
loyal father, his longtime friend. He thought of all the men whom
he had known and with whom for good or ill he had worked.

He wandered into the armory with its rich trophies, weapons
that had been wielded by the leaders and the enemies of the Kozaks.
He chose for his own use a diamond-studded sword which Soliman
the Magnificent had captured from a Doge of Venice and had presented to a Khan of the Crimea. He had taken it himself in battle.
He picked out the dagger of Doroshenko, the last Hetman who
dared to form an independent policy. The weapons spoke of the
past and present; they pointed the way to the future.

At dawn he called the officers to the great hall. His staff knew
what was coming. There were about one hundred present, as by
lighted torches in the gray light of a November dawn Mazeppa
rose and in measured words announced that he was leading his
troops to the Swedish camp to join the invaders and to rescue
Ukraine from the Muscovites. The news fell like a bombshell but
the Hetman's orders still rang on.

He named Colonel Chechel commander of Baturyn and gave
him 5,000 Kozaks. He ordered him to hold the fortress to the
end and never surrender. He named a German, Colonel Konigsen,
to command the artillery. In no uncertain terms he charged the
officers to blow up the palace and the fortifications rather than to
surrender to the Muscovites and the officers swore to die rather than
to yield. He promised to relieve the garrison in a few days on his
return.

Then all was ready. The column was formed. Mazeppa took
his seat in his coach with six white horses and his favorite mounts
beside it. When the last man had crossed the drawbridge, the bridge
was raised, the gates were shut and locked, and Baturyn was ready
for a siege.

How many men did Mazeppa take with him. Estimates vary
widely. Bardili, writing in 1730, says that he had some 20-30,000.
Menshikov reported that he had with him only some 1500, mercenaries and personal friends. The Russians have always tried to

picture Mazeppa as a ruined man. The Ukrainians have been inclined to credit him with larger forces although many deserted when
the pro-Muscovites learned his plans.

It was now November 4. After a day's march, the army bivouacked
on the bank of the Desna. The next day they crossed the river.
Mazeppa had said not a word about his plans after he had left the
meeting of the officers. Now he ordered the men to form a great
semicircle. He mounted his horse and rode into the centre with
Orlyk and Voynarovsky. Then he dismounted and began to speak:

"We are now, thank God, on the right bank of the Desna.
Do you think I am leading you to battle against the glorious Swedish
army? No, never. We are marching against the hereditary enemy
of our people, the Tsar of Moscow, who has sworn to destroy our
liberties and to make of us, free Kozaks, the slaves of his house.
Do you consent to that?

"I have more than once spoken to the Tsar and he has told
me his plans. He wishes to suppress the post of Hetman, to dis-
band the Kozak regiments and replace them with hired troops.

"I have tried often to dissuade him from this deadly course which
is so dangerous for the Ukrainian people. My intervention has been
useless. It has served only to turn the Tsar against me and he has
finally ended by putting me under the orders of Menshikov.

"Brothers, our hour is come. Let us profit by the occasion. Let
us take vengeance on the Muscovites.

"Let us take vengeance for the great violence which they have
used so long against us; let us take vengeance for all their brutalities and their injustices. Let us guard hereafter our liberty and the
rights of the Kozaks against all their attacks.

"The hour is come to throw off their hated yoke and to make
our Ukraine a free and independent country.

"That is why I have decided to go over with you to the glorious
King of Sweden, to Charles. He promises to respect our rights and
liberties; he swears to defend us by every means in his power
against the assaults of Moscow; he is willing to guarantee the

independence of Ukraine. The first power of Europe, France, is with us. Will you follow me?

"Brothers, the will of God is not shown to sinners. But whatever God is preparing for us, we cannot any longer tolerate the Muscovite yoke. What is the value of a people which is unable to face the danger that threatens it? Are they not lowered to the rank of animals without feelings and are they not worthy of the contempt of other peoples? Between the Tsar and us the battle is on.

"Now, brothers, if we must die, it is better to die with arms in hand than to finish our days under torture."

Mazeppa was a master of oratory and of charm. His speech moved his little army and for the moment he was cheered even by those officers and men whom he suspected of pro-Muscovite sentiments. Then the troops were reformed and the march was resumed.

The Hetman sent Orlyk and Lomykovsky ahead to reach the Swedish outposts as soon as possible. They found in the village of Orlykivka two Swedish regiments under the command of Colonels Hielm and Hillenstiern. These had recently driven off an attack by Menshikov's cavalry. Now to their surprise they saw two high Kozak officers approaching. They at once suspected that Peter had thought up a new act of treachery, when the envoys told them that Mazeppa and his men were coming to join the Swedes.

After a short parley, the Swedes were half-convinced but to make assurance sure, they sent back with the two Kozaks an Italian officer who had previously known Mazeppa. He returned in a short time with the confirmation of the amazing news.

A little later, Mazeppa, his staff and his troops appeared. This startled the officers, now that they were face to face with such a large body of Kozaks. They passed them through their lines, while they sent messengers back to report to the King. The Hetman and his staff spent the night with the Swedish officers, while the men bivouacked in the open fields.

The next days were spent in preparing for a ceremonial meeting of the two armies. Both Charles and Mazeppa were sticklers for etiquette. Both knew the value of a pageant and both were eager to carry it through without a hitch. The General Osaul Maksymovych went on to the King's headquarters, while Mazeppa remained at Orlykivka and saw to his regret that a certain number of his officers and men took this opportunity to desert to the Muscovites.

On November 8 at nine o'clock in the morning, all was ready. Charles, wearing the decoration of the Grand Cordon of the Holy Spirit which had been given to his ancestor Gustavus Adolphus by Richelieu himself, took his position among his most distinguished officers, while the crack regiments of his army were drawn up at attention in a great semicircle.

Into this moved a detachment of Kozak scouts. Then came the leading officers of Mazeppa's staff, Orlyk, Lomykovsky and Apostol, so soon to desert. Next came Voynarovsky carrying the horse-tail standard and the mace of the Hetman and finally the dignified figure of Mazeppa himself on horseback with a detachment of his guard.

At the proper distance, the Hetman dismounted and advanced on foot to greet the King. The two sovereigns met formally. There was nothing to indicate obeisance or subservience. In sonorous Latin Mazeppa commenced a long speech of greeting. He listed without an error the complicated titles of the Swedish King and then expressed his thanks and those of the Host for the great assistance of His Majesty in aiding Ukraine to throw off the yoke of Moscow.

At the end of the speech, Charles made a low bow to the Hetman and then in deference to his age and dignity, he bade him be seated and remained standing himself, while he returned the greeting. This was an unprecedented act for Charles who had never shown such courtesy to the lesser sovereigns whom he had met or placed in power. His greeting of the Hetman of Ukraine was in marked contrast to the almost contemptuous courtesy with which he had met King Stanislaw, his puppet King. Everything bespoke his respect and admiration for the aged Hetman and the slightest details had been prepared to avoid injuring the dignity and sensibilities of Mazeppa.

In a sense, this was the crowning event of the career of Ivan Mazeppa. Received as Hetman of an independent Ukraine by Charles XII, the King of the Swedes, Goths and Vandals and the leading military figure of the day, the Hetman had achieved something that had not been granted even to Bohdan Khmelnytsky or any of his successors, the recognition of the sovereignty of his people by a sovereign of the West. No Ukrainian had yet received such an honor since the days of the Grand Princes of Kiev centuries before and it was a symbolic expression of something of real importance. At long last Ukraine was returning to the society of Western Europe.

CHAPTER EIGHTEEN

THE VENGEANCE OF THE TSAR

Mazeppa's junction with Charles XII could not long be concealed. In fact it was hardly a day before Peter heard the startling news which upset all his plans. He could scarcely believe his own ears.

As Voynarovsky had correctly reported, Menshikov was on his way to Baturyn so as to be present when Mazeppa breathed his last and to prevent any unfavorable movement among the Kozak officers who might seize the opportunity to vent their spite on the Muscovite regime. As he approached, he heard to his surprise of the Hetman's wild ride back to Baturyn and then he met Colonel Annenkov with Mazeppa's letter of apology for his nephew. Rumors which indicated that Mazeppa was on his way to join the Swedes led him to turn aside from Borzna and go straight to Baturyn where he arrived on November 5 at about the same time that Mazeppa reached the camp of Charles. At about the same time Prince Dimitry Golitsyn, the Governor of Kiev, also appeared at Baturyn and ordered Chechel to admit a Muscovite regiment.

The Muscovites were not admitted. They were told that this required the order of the Hetman. In an effort to mislead them, Chechel said that the Hetman had gone to look for Peter near the village of Korop. Of course this excuse impressed no one, the more so as they could learn from Annenkov what officers had been with Mazeppa when he left the fortress.

In view of the overwhelming evidence as to what Mazeppa had done, Menshikov sent a message to Peter to announce the treachery of the Hetman and he added that it would be a good piece of strategy for the Tsar to emphasize the evil that Mazeppa had done to his people and to denounce him as an enemy of the "Little Russians." He urged the Tsar to enter Ukraine himself and to appeal to all those classes which were dissatisfied with the existing order by laying all the blame upon the Hetman. He reckoned on the fact that there were many who would not stop to think that it had been the necessity for satisfying the Tsar's demands that had forced Mazeppa into some of his more unpopular policies and that these people would jump at the opportunity to accept the Tsar's word as to the better times that were coming.

The reports of Menshikov seemed to Peter at first utterly fantastic. He had persistently refused to believe any of the accusations against the Hetman and he had relied upon him to keep the Kozak officers in check, for he had decided that they were the cause of the discontent that he knew was rife in the country. Now his plans were upset and the Tsar plunged into one of his wild and uncontrollable fits of anger.

He began to issue manifesto after manifesto against the Hetman and his language became more and more virulent. The full force of Muscovite invective was directed against his former friend. Mazeppa was now a dog and a Judas, a bloodthirsty piece of vermin and other terms even more unprintable. Peter's innate vulgarity and cruelty rose to the surface and he not only called the Hetman all the abusive terms of which he could think but he determined to prepare for him special tortures, once he got him in his hands.

His first task was to select a new Hetman. It was impossible now for him to abolish the post. All the traditions that for more than a century had been connected with the position would remain associated with Ivan Mazeppa and Peter wanted to prevent that. His problem then was to secure a new Hetman who would be subservient to his will but he did not intend to allow his new choice to possess any real power.

He had in his camp a certain number of Kozak officers. Some of these were the extreme pro-Muscovites; others had been jealous of Mazeppa and had left him; still others were officers of the regiments which came from cities already occupied by Peter's troops and these last had had no opportunity to get away because of Mazeppa's dilatory policy before the final break. Peter ordered all these to meet at Hlukhiv on the borders of Ukraine where they could be easily overawed by the Muscovite army.

In calling this meeting Peter announced that Mazeppa, the new Judas, had made an agreement with the King of Sweden and Leszczynski "to deliver the Little Russian country to Polish domination, and to turn over to the Union (the Uniat Church) the Church of God and its glorious convents and monasteries." Then he had the effrontery to add: "Since it is on us that there lies the duty of protecting the Little Russian land, we will extend over it our paternal hand. We will save Little Russia from enslavement and ruin. We will not allow its divine churches to be dishonored. So we appeal to all the chiefs and colonels; we adjure them not to lend an ear to the deceptive seductions of the old Hetman, this traitor, but to come to the defence of our Great Russian troops against the enemy."

At the same time he abolished all the taxes that the Hetman had levied and announced that he was substituting the Muscovite system. It was contrary to the treaties between the Tsar and the Host but what of that? Peter was gambling on the fact that the average Ukrainian peasant would see only the abolition of the old annoyances and would not for the present realize that he had jumped from the frying pan into the fire with the additional inconvenience that from now on the money would be entirely removed from the country and would not be spent on any of the institutions which Mazeppa had so bountifully supported.

His next object was to get possession of Baturyn and here again he was favored by the delay of Mazeppa and Charles in entering action. Their formal meeting was followed by a series of banquets to celebrate the new Ukrainian-Swedish friendship and they wasted a few days in forming a joint plan of action. The two leaders were constantly together, they conversed in fluent Latin with all of the flattery and compliments of the day and the King was charmed by his new friend.

In the meanwhile Peter was not idle. He sent Menshikov who had been advancing with a few troops enough men to storm the city.

Prince Golitsyn arrived with soldiers on November 10 and Menshikov's troops appeared the next day. They tried to cross the Seym to
attack the city but Konigsen's artillery destroyed all bridges erected
near the fortress.

The garrison was obviously taking seriously Mazeppa's orders
to hold out to the end or until he returned. Neither the garrison
nor the Muscovites knew when this would be. At the same time
attempts at storming the city were resolutely repulsed.

Then treason accomplished what force could not. An officer of
the Pryluky Regiment named Nos deserted and succeeded in reach-
ing Menshikov's camp. He brought word of a secret passage which
led into the fortress and might thus break the deadlock. He was
given a picked body of men and with this he succeeded in penetrat-
ing the interior at the same time that the attack on the walls was
repeated. The garrison, not expecting to find the enemy within
the walls, was startled and lost the initiative and after a desperate
battle, the Muscovite troops gained possession of the coveted capital
of the Hetman. Their losses had been heavy, for some 3,000 men
were killed. About 1,000 of the defenders succeeded in escaping at the last moment and making their way to Mazeppa.

Once the Russians were in control, a wild butchery commenced.
Peter had given orders that even in case of surrender not a single
person in the city should be left alive. Soldiers and civilians, men,
women and children were massacred in cold blood, with the troops
taking care to ravish and rape and torture all of the young women.
Nothing so thrilled Peter as the possibility of giving free reign to his
vengeance and his lust for blood and his men went to work with a
will to satisfy him. Then in order to spread terror in still wider
circles, the bodies of many of the officers were nailed to planks and
thrown into the Seym so that they could float downstream and be
mute testimony to Peter's victory.

The carnage went on throughout November 13 and 14. The
commandant, Colonel Chechel, and Colonel Konigsen were reserved
for special tortures at the pleasure of His Majesty. This was good
for Konigsen for he had been badly wounded and despite the efforts

of the Tsar's physicians to keep him alive for execution, he passed away. Chechel was not so fortunate. He had been unable to find death, although he had been in the centre of the most desperate fighting and he was carried off to the headquarters of the Tsar, where the monarch and his executioners used all of their ingenuity in developing new modes of torture. It is conservatively estimated that over 15,000 men, women and children were killed in cold blood during these two days so that the Tsar and Menshikov could properly celebrate their glorious victory.

The massacre made news. Such a complete holocaust of victims was not in the tradition of the eighteenth century. The Paris newspapers published detailed accounts of the Muscovite barbarism. It was a striking comment on Peter's efforts to pose as a civilized European ruler and it brought home to many of the Western statesmen, for a while at least, the real significance of the entrance of Muscovite Russia into the European political arena.

Baturyn was burned to the ground and levelled. The banners and the artillery of Mazeppa, his great collection of works of art and his treasury and library passed into the hands of Menshikov, although the largest part was destroyed in the burning of the city. Nothing was left of Baturyn and when the Muscovites finally withdrew, they left behind them a pile of smoking ashes and heaps of unburied corpses which polluted the air for weeks and months.

The capture and destruction of Baturyn and its population produced the desired effect. It had been intended as a warning and coming as it did, barely a week after Mazeppa had joined the Swedes, it impressed many lukewarm patriots into believing in the invulnerability of the Tsar. They had not been prepared for war and this sudden defeat of the Ukrainian cause seemed to them a bad omen.

It impressed also the Kozak officers who were called to Hlukhiv. It was made clear to them that they had no voice in the selection of a new Hetman. They would have preferred Colonel Polubotok of Chernyhiv. Polubotok was a sincere, loyal and capable Kozak officer who was later as Acting Hetman to die in the dungeons of St. Petersburg for defending the rights of his position but that was still in the future. Now he seemed too able and dangerous for Peter, who feared that he might develop some of the independence of Mazeppa. Peter selected Colonel Ivan Skoropadsky of the Starodub Regiment. He was old and weak and though he was on the whole patriotic and his relatives were with Mazeppa, his failure to block the entrance of Infland into Starodub endeared him to Peter. He seemed that type of harmless figurehead that suited the Tsar's policy and would not go beyond his orders. The Tsar called for his election and the few assembled officers elected him "since it was the will of the Tsar." Skoropadsky then took an oath to reveal to the Russian authorities any information that he might secure about Mazeppa, to have no contact with him, and to report any one who showed the slightest sign of sympathy for the old Hetman. Even this did not seem sufficient and the Tsar placed his seat in Hlukhiv and gave him a Muscovite agent to watch his every step and to pass on even the slightest action which he might take. The new Hetman had no power either over the affairs of the Host or the Ukrainian people.

As part of the ceremonies for the installation of the new Hetman, Peter had Mazeppa hanged in effigy, since he had not succeeded in laying his hands upon his enemy. A scaffold was erected in front of the Cathedral in Hlukhiv, a manikin was brought in under heavy guard and then Menshikov and Chancellor Golovkin mounted the scaffold and tore off the decoration of St. Andrew from the neck of the figure. The executioner read aloud the Tsar's list of charges and the manikin was hung and then dragged with jeers through the streets of Hlukhiv.

Peter's vengeance was still not satisfied. He wanted a more striking demonstration of Mazeppa's condemnation and he called upon the Orthodox bishops in Ukraine to furnish it. He was perhaps scarcely prepared for the willingness of the high ecclesiastics to turn against their former patron and benefactor. On November 23, the Novgorod Protopope A. Zarutsky, a former friend of Mazeppa, pronounced a formal excommunication and cursing of the Hetman with all of the pageantry that the Orthodox Church could produce.

Through the Church rang out the cry "To the traitor and perjurer Mazeppa anathema." The cry was taken up by the clergy, by the Kozak officers who were forced to attend, by the terrorized population forced on by the Muscovite troops who were in full military control of the situation.

On the same day a still more elaborate service was held in the Cathedral of the Repose in Moscow. The Tsarevich Alexis, soon himself to perish at his father's hands, represented the Tsar. The anathema was pronounced by no less an ecclesiastic than the Acting Patriarch Stefan Yavorsky. He had been a protégé of Mazeppa and thanks to the Hetman's influence, he had become the head of the Academy in Kiev and then had had rapid promotion in Moscow and was now the Archbishop of Ryazan. He had been the teacher of Orlyk and had composed one of the most famous panegyrics of the Hetman. Now he turned on his former patron and condemned him as a "venomous and cunning serpent, a fox, a devil, a Judas, a hypocrite, a second Cain." Warming up to his subject, he went on, describing him as a "furious wolf, hiding under the mask of a tender lamb, sweet in words, but cruel in actions. Hurl at me your poisoned darts, traitor for whom hell is waiting."

The clergy and Peter were not content with condemning Mazeppa in the present and damning him in the future. They attempted to read him out of the past. He had been the great patron of the Ukrainian Orthodox, a benefactor of the Church, a great builder and restorer. They went over all their buildings, their shrines, their decorations, and wherever they found a plaque or an inscription that bore the name of the Hetman, they carefully chiselled it out or painted it over. Teofan Prokopovych, the then Rector of the Academy, revised his tragicomedy *Vladimir* which had been dedicated to Mazeppa and reworked it in honor of Peter and for this service, he became Archbishop of Novgorod. The clergy diligently spread the story that the Hetman had become a Catholic and there was no slander, no scandal which they were not willing to repeat.

The Kozak officers followed the example of the clergy. Peter made liberal promises of pardon and of amnesty to all who would abandon the old Hetman. He confiscated Mazeppa's estates and those of his followers and distributed them among Muscovites and Ukrainians who had remained loyal to him. Prince Golitsyn received 25,000 rubles from the treasury of Mazeppa for his efforts during the siege of Baturyn. Menshikov secured 6,000 ducats and other high officials were similarly rewarded.

At the same time the Tsar pursued ruthlessly all those who might be suspected of sympathizing with the Hetman and he was determined that no one who was closely connected with him should remain alive. He set up at Lebedin near Kharkiv a special section of the Chancellery of the Ambassadors, as the torture chambers were euphemistically called, and special appliances for their work were brought from Moscow. Here for weeks at a time, the Tsar, Menshikov and Romodanovsky wracked their brains for new and more painful methods of torture, for the use of the knout, the breaking on the wheel, the burning with red hot irons. The Tsar took part in all these tortures as a part of his personal obligation and as a proof that he was the progressive leader of the Muscovites.

It is known that over 900 persons actually died under the tortures and this does not include those who were later executed in one form or another. The total number of victims has never been recorded but the general trend of the nightmare can well be seen in the words written later in the *History of the Rus'*: "And now, if as our Lord said in the Gospel, each drop of blood shed on the earth will be expiated by those who shed it, what expiation awaits the executioners of the Ukrainian people? They shed their blood in floods and why? Because they wished to be free and to know a better life in their own country. Were these not ideas common to all humanity?"

Peter's successors continued his tradition. The Great Russians did everything possible to make the Hetman the classic figure of the traitor in Russian history. No Russian historian can be fair to him and year by year the Russian Orthodox Church until the Revolution and the downfall of the monarchy continued to proclaim the anathemas which were hurled against Ivan Mazeppa by the minions of Peter.

Peter's rage knew no bounds but there was good reason for it. Mazeppa was endeavoring to restore the liberty of Ukraine. His attempt meant the thwarting of the holy will of the Tsar, the defiance of the Third Rome, the centre of the world, and the checking of the Muscovite desire for expansion. The fate of Moscow hung upon the outcome of the struggle and Mazeppa came too uncomfortably near to victory. All through the following months, Georg Johann Freiherr von Kayserling, the Prussian envoy at the court of Peter, never failed to mention in his reports that conditions were not good in the Russian army. He stressed the Russian disorganization, the fact that Peter was maintaining control by terror. The Tsar had the uneasy feeling that that terror might defeat its own purpose but he never wavered from his course.

Hence the strange paradox and the bitter enmity to the Hetman. In one and the same breath, the Russian historians stress the futility of Mazeppa's efforts, they magnify the isolation in which he found himself, and they paint the deep rascality of a man who was trying to shatter the unity of the Russian Empire. If Mazeppa were an isolated figure, there would be no need to condemn him so bitterly. If he were the mouthpiece of a region and a people, he was dangerous but the Russians wish to have it both ways at the same time. It throws into relief the position of the Hetman and the magnitude of his hopes and efforts. Could he succeed in securing the commensurate results? That was the question.

CHAPTER NINETEEN

THE STRUGGLE FOR FREEDOM

The news of the fall of Baturyn came as a blow to both Charles XII and Mazeppa. The effect was more pronounced upon the officers and men who had come with Mazeppa to the Swedish camp. It accelerated their desertion and many even returned to take service with Peter.

The Hetman was forced to realize that he had made one great mistake. If he had ever dreamed that he could raise the whole of Ukraine by his mere word, he was cruelly disillusioned. Throughout the whole of the Northern War, his policy had been an unwavering and apparently sincere support of the Tsar. He had stressed this and he had dimmed the hopes of many of his most faithful and patriotic followers. Now with the campaign under way and under the additional handicap of the destruction of Baturyn, he had to reverse his course and convince his people of his loyalty and sincerity to his new ally. He saw clearly that he had to prepare the minds of his followers and do under heavy odds the work that he had felt himself forced to neglect.

A change in his own methods of action was no less necessary. He had held his post for nearly two decades by his ability to plan and work in secret, to thwart hidden opposition without arousing the suspicions of the Tsar. Now as the commander of the Kozak forces fighting for their independence, frankness and openness were required. It meant the change of the habits of a lifetime and it took him time to become fully conscious of his new role.

This was the more necessary because of the character of the Swedish King. He shared his military plans with none of his staff. They had only to obey his orders without questioning as to their fundamental meaning and their purpose. Outside of this, he was as frank and direct as the Russians had been crafty and scheming. Mazeppa had no need for that flattery and indirection which had served him so well during his long life. When Charles asked a question, he wanted a direct and unequivocal answer and the Hetman had to learn how to satisfy him. It did not prove as hard as he had expected.

The two leaders coordinated their plans and two days after the fall of Baturyn, Charles and Mazeppa led their troops across the Desna and into the interior of the country. The Russians tried to interfere with the crossing but the combination of Swedish engineering skill and the Kozak knowledge of the country speedily eliminated their efforts and the enemy withdraw discomfitted.

It was just a week later that the armies passed the still smouldering ruins of Baturyn. The air was foul with the thousands of decaying corpses. The sight nearly broke the heart of the old Hetman. He turned to Orlyk who was riding with him and said:

"Our beginning is unlucky. I see that the Lord has not blessed our plan. And yet God is my witness that I could not act otherwise. How could I stand any longer the perpetual injustice done to my people, contemplate any longer the violation of our rights and liberties, let them prepare under my eyes the ruin and destruction of Ukraine!

"It is true we were formerly allies to the Tsars of Moscow; but we joined them of our free will, guided only by the brotherhood of our religions. The Muscovites have abused our confidence and now, free people that we are, we denounce this alliance. Alas! I am afraid that our plans will become more difficult to realize. Ukraine, terrorized by the fate of Baturyn, will perhaps be afraid to take our part."

On leaving his capital, the Hetman had dreamed of bringing Charles to it and of sharing with him his supplies. Now that was impossible but the armies moved to Mazeppa's estates at Bakhmach and it was there that he summoned the Kozak leaders to meet him. To those who came Mazeppa gave a solemn oath that he would not give up the struggle until Ukraine was really free.

By the end of the month with winter rapidly approaching, the Swedish armies occupied Romny and Hadyach without serious fighting and prepared to spend the winter in this area, although

Charles did not want to allow the weather to interfere in his plans. He did not appreciate the severity of the continental winter and the depth of the snow which was far greater than any that he had ever encountered.

As a matter of fact the winter of 1708-1709 was one of the most terrible on record. It began early and continued without any interruption. The mercury sank to unprecedented lows and the snow was unusually deep. The Swedish troops were ill prepared to face it.

When Charles was crossing the Desna in the middle of November, he was shivering in his light uniform. Mazeppa, anxious for his health, presented him with a fur coat of silver fox and the King was glad to put it on. But not for long. As soon as he noticed the discomfort of his soldiers, he at once discarded it, for he made it a matter of pride to share all the hardships of his men and he was not going to violate his principles for a little thing like a fur coat. The soldiers noticed it. The sight of their King suffering from the cold as they were took their minds from their own troubles and Charles performed the apparent miracle of maintaining the morale of his troops under the most impossible conditions.

Still the cold did take a terrible toll from the small army. At one time there were over 4,000 men in the hospitals which he established in Hadyach. Men died of freezing and starvation and their loss was irreplaceable, now that Loewenhaupt had been defeated and no reinforcements were to be expected from Sweden.

In one sense this enforced inactivity brought its own benefits. A war of words commenced, as Charles and Mazeppa issued manifesto after manifesto calling for a free Ukraine and emphasizing the unspeakable brutalities that Peter was inflicting upon the people. They repudiated the repeated statement of the Tsar that they were planning to turn the country over to the Poles and Roman Catholics. Peter on his part went ahead with his appeals to religious prejudice and to the egotism and greed of the officers, as he gave the estates of Mazeppa and his friends to his personal friends and those who were ready to serve him.

The appeal to the religious brotherhood of the Muscovites and Ukrainians was his strongest weapon. The Kozaks had always been devoted to the cause of Orthodoxy. That had been their rallying cry a century earlier against the Poles and the sight of their Hetman in an alliance with a Protestant prince was enough to deter many from joining him, even though they grumbled at the elimination of their own special Ukrainian customs. They preferred to be Orthodox with Peter and to avoid contacts with possible heretics.

At the same time Peter's atrocities were the best recruiting agent for Mazeppa. Even the Swedes had expected that the Tsar would endeavor by kind treatment to win friends and solidify the Ukrainian population behind him. That was not Peter's idea. He was going to destroy not only Ivan Mazeppa but every one who dared to criticize his own rule. As a result it was not long before Mazeppa's forces began to grow again. Officers and ordinary Kozaks who had slipped away in the early days of November began to find their way back to an army where they could be sure of stern but just treatment. Villages which were being ravaged by the Muscovite soldiers poured out to fight for their liberties and safety. In this respect time was on the side of the Hetman and by spring he had a larger force than he had had in November or than even seemed possible after the fall of Baturyn.

This slow but persistent swing in the temper of the population often proved embarrassing to Charles and the Swedes. They came from a thoroughly nationalistic people. The unity of Sweden had been forged through the centuries and they expected the same of Ukraine. The forthright character of the King could not comprehend the attitude of the terrorized and confused population.

To Charles any one in Ukraine who refused to recognize the power of the Hetman was simply to be put down as a traitor. He treated the population fairly and humanely but he was inclined to be inexorable when he was called upon to deal with those waverers who still felt some sort of allegiance to the Tsar. On the other hand as he showed at the town of Vepryk, he was only too ready to pardon offenders, if they would come back to their proper allegiance and do their part in the efforts to liberate their country.

Many partisan bands sprang up throughout the area. In some cases these were composed of the more fanatically pro-Muscovite Ukrainians but there can be little doubt that the greater part of them were men who had been sent into the area by Peter to prey upon small Swedish detachments away from their bases on various missions.

In the late winter Charles and his army moved east into the Land of Free Communes. This was northeast of Ukraine proper on the road to Moscow. Its population was largely Ukrainian but it was technically under Muscovite sovereignty. Hetman after Hetman had petitioned the Tsar to add this territory to their domains. It had been the dream of Khmelnytsky to acquire it. The Ukrainians after the Ruin had swarmed into the region but at the same time Great Russians came down from the north and none of the Tsars saw fit to give up the area although for decades Muscovite rule was almost conspicuously absent and there were constant clashes between the two elements of the population.

The policy of Charles was put to a severe test in this region. He seems to have accepted this region as Muscovite territory and allowed his soldiers to behave as in a conquered country. With his legalistic conception of nationality, he paid little attention as to whether a certain village was Muscovite or Ukrainian. As a result he encountered distinct hostility and the greater part of the Ukrainians who actively opposed him came from this area.

The advance of Charles into this area showed that a march on Moscow was impracticable in the deep snow and the freezing cold. His armies were shrinking in numbers and he was beginning to suffer for the lack of trained infantry for even now there was no hope that he could organize and train a Ukrainian infantry force that was up to his own standards. They still were organized as irregular Kozak cavalry and their tactics were still those that they had found useful for more than a century.

On the other hand, with his return to Ukraine proper, Charles was still more open to the broadening of his allies to include the aid of Turkey and the Crimean Tatars. He began to appreciate the possibilities of this new theatre of war but to exploit it properly, he needed the control of the Dnieper. With this in mind he returned to the neighborhood of Hadyach.

Here both he and Mazeppa were cheered by the decision of the Zaporozhian Sich to throw in its lot with him. The Sich no longer had its former power but its Kozaks enjoyed a disproportionate respect from the entire population. They were the most turbulent of all the Kozak formations and were bitter against the Muscovite infringement of their ancient liberties. Mazeppa himself from his own experience could testify to this. They were however equally opposed to the efforts of the Hetman and the regimental commanders to fit them into the regular Kozak forces and they refused to cooperate in the measures that were being taken to organize the country. Still when Mazeppa made the final break and openly took the field against Peter, their old hostility to him was gradually reduced and they began to think of helping him against the common enemy.

During the month of March, Peter made every effort to shake the Zaporozhians out of the neutrality which they had assumed in the beginning. He sent them a series of ambassadors with elaborate presents to induce them to take up arms in his behalf. A little later he sent an Archimandrite of the Orthodox Church to stir up their religious fanaticism and turn it against Mazeppa. To counteract these missions, Mazeppa sent Orlyk, the General Judge Chuykevych, Colonel Mokiyevsky of Kiev and Myrovych, one of his most ardent partisans, to the Sich. These were to plead the cause of the Hetman, to appeal to the Sich love of liberty and to point out how an independent Ukraine could foster those ideals to which the Zaporozhian Sich was so strongly attached.

On March 25, 1709, the Sich held a general assembly to decide on a future course of action. The representatives of both the Tsar and Mazeppa were present and each pleaded their case. Orlyk even had a special letter from Mazeppa for the occasion. In addition, the Khan of the Crimea also had sent a letter, urging the Sich to take the side of Charles. Apparently the plans for a great anti-Muscovite confederation were beginning to take shape.

The decisive speech was made by Kost Hordiyenko, the Koshovy Otaman or the actual administrative head of the Sich. In impassioned words, he begged the Kozaks to be true to their principles of liberty, to forget their former quarrels with Mazeppa and to seize this priceless opportunity of securing themselves against Muscovite oppression by aiding Charles and Mazeppa. His words carried the day. The Sich abandoned its policy of neutrality and voted enthusiastically to send envoys to Charles and to join him.

For the Zaporozhians to think was to act. Hordiyenko immediately wrote a letter to the King and placed the Sich under his protection. Then he led a selected delegation to the Swedish camp. On its way it captured over one hundred Muscovite prisoners and arrived with them on March 30 at Velyky Budyshchi where Mazeppa was staying.

On April 5, Mazeppa met the delegation and entertained them royally. He sent a force of 2,000 Kozaks under two colonels to meet them as they approached and to escort them to his camp and then he entertained them at Dikanka, the former estate of Kochubey. Here there was another large reception and the Hetman spared no pains to impress the Kozaks and make them feel at home.

He received Hordiyenko in his full regalia and after his speech Hordiyenko replied in the name of the Sich. He expressed the appreciation of the Sich for the noble motives that had inspired the Hetman to undertake this struggle for liberty and he assured him that the Zaporozhians would cooperate faithfully, until full independence was achieved. He added, however, that he wished the Hetman to take an oath to cooperate with them and to maintain their old rights and privileges. Mazeppa agreed and a definite treaty was drawn up between the Hetman and the Zaporozhians. Because of ill health Mazeppa signed this in his quarters and the Zaporozhians took the oath in the local church.

Then came another banquet at which the mission was encouraged to eat and to drink their fill. The Zaporozhians had always been noted for their hospitality. They freely entertained all visitors and the Hetman went out of his way to stress the fact that the new Ukrainian regime was living up to the glorious traditions of the Sich.

The next day he formally presented Hordiyenko and the delegation to King Charles. It was another of those great demonstrations of the power and dignity of the Swedish King. His secretary delivered a flowery speech in Latin and Soldan, one of his staff who knew Ukrainian, translated it. Charles distributed presents and gave them another banquet. At this time the Zaporozhians presented the text for another treaty guaranteeing their liberties. This was a treaty between Charles, Mazeppa and the Zaporozhians covering the same ground as the earlier one with Mazeppa. Charles issued a royal confirmation of it.

Well satisfied, the delegation started back to the Sich. As they passed Poltava, one of the few places in central and southern Ukraine where the Muscovites still had a garrison, the Muscovite troops opened fire upon them. The delegates replied and the Kozak sharpshooters picked off several Muscovite officers who dared to show themselves above the ramparts.

After its return to the Sich, the members of the delegation scattered. They had brought back with them letters from Mazeppa to both the Khan and the Sultan and selected envoys went off to deliver them and to formulate new plans for bringing both the Tatars and the Turks to the aid of the Kozaks and Charles.

The accession of the Sich was a great victory. All those people who had been lukewarm in their support of the Hetman began to change their minds. The Sich was noted for its independence and its Orthodoxy. If it had decided to come out on the side of the Hetman, it was obvious that the propaganda of Peter was false and that the Hetman was the representative of all that was best in the country. Recruits began to pour in and when spring came, the country began to be really aroused. The winter of doubt was passing and everything promised well for the summer campaign.

This deliberate preference of the Sich for Charles and Mazeppa infuriated Peter and he determined at all costs to take a new vengeance. It enraged him that his envoys had been deliberately spurned and that any organized force should dare to question his imperial will. Besides he knew what this might mean to the already wavering Ukrainians and he looked with apprehension at the opening of direct relations between Charles and the countries to the south. Once that were open, the Swedes would no longer be isolated but they would be in touch with the maritime countries of the West in a new theatre which he regarded as his own special domain.

He sent Menshikov with a large force of men down the Dnieper. Some travelled by land and some in boats to the Sich headquarters. The place was lightly garrisoned as always when the Kozaks were at war. There was left only a small group to protect the supplies stored on the islands. The main body of the Zaporozhians were scattered around the area, attacking the Muscovite garrisons and cutting off isolated detachments of Muscovite troops.

Some of the men under Colonel Yakovlev soon succeeded in capturing Fort Kodak, one of the outposts. This fortress had played an important part in the long wars between the Kozaks and the Poles but it had lost most of its importance. The detachment then moved on to Kamenny Zaton and from here demanded the surrender of the Sich. The summons was declined.

An assault on the islands failed and the Kozaks captured a number of prisoners and executed some Muscovite officers in return for the massacre of Baturyn.

Then on May 18, treachery succeeded again where direct assault failed. A Kozak officer named Halahan was with the attacking force. He had gone with Mazeppa in the beginning but had been one of the deserters and he was trying to secure the favor of the Muscovites by special services. He succeeded through his knowledge of the country in landing with a Muscovite detachment on the islands and again as at Baturyn in subjecting the Kozaks to attacks from within and without.

The garrison consisted of only three hundred men and faced by superior force, they were induced to surrender on the condition that their lives would be spared. Of course this promise, even after it had been strengthened by an oath in the Sich church, meant nothing to the Muscovites. Once the Kozaks had surrendered, they were seized and put to the torture. All the devices that had been used in the punishment of the Baturyn garrison were again employed with further refinements of cruelty, and if the ensuing massacres were smaller, it was only because of a lesser number of possible victims.

Once the Sich was in Muscovite hands, its wealth and its armaments were seized and distributed to Peter's favorites. Menshikov sent out detachments of cavalry to track down small Kozak bands which were absent from the Sich or were trying to escape from the debacle. All who were captured were tortured and so were any unsuspecting Kozaks who were returning to their former stronghold. The only Zaporozhians who escaped were those who were able to reach Mazeppa's forces or went into exile in Turkey rather than surrender. For the first time in a century and a half the Sich was in the hands of its enemies.

During this winter and spring the cooperation of Charles and Mazeppa surprised all their friends. The young King, always a stickler for the courtesy due him, came to feel a warm personal regard for the aged Hetman and Mazeppa, always the courtier, turned many a graceful compliment to his companion who perhaps did not always appreciate the point.

For example, one day near Valky in the Land of Free Communes, Mazeppa remarked to Charles that the army was only eight leagues from Asia. Charles, who had taken Alexander the Great as his model, was greatly impressed and to follow up his comment, the Hetman remarked that there had been recently discovered in Ukraine a monument erected by Alexander. That evening Colonel Gyllenbrook told the Hetman that it was dangerous to pass such jokes with Charles who was so eager to achieve glory.

Mazeppa's words were not merely flattery. The Hetman from his knowledge of the Latin classics was only too well aware that the ancient geographers treated the eastern boundary of Ukraine, the line of the Don, as the boundary between Europe and Asia. There was a deeper political side to his remark and a definite allusion to the barbarism of Peter and his associates.

Another phase of the relationship between Charles and Mazeppa was more unconscious and more vague but equally real. Mazeppa had been trying to make Ukraine a really Western state with a Western form of government. He had long known the weakness in the old form of the Kozak organization exactly as he understood the defects of the system of the Zaporozhians. The system worked in the hands of a strong ruler like Khmelnytsky but since that time the final authority, as he well knew, had been in the hands of a foreigner. How could it be recovered practically?

He knew his life was running out. He had been rejuvenated by his effort to win the freedom of his country but he was well aware that that was not enough. He wanted to create a new system, something different from that in Poland and in Moscow. He apparently was dreaming of some sort of a hereditary Hetmanate, perhaps something similar to the system of Charles which could be applied to the liberties of the Host and serve as a basis for a new order.

His conversations with Charles, with the Swedish officers, with Orlyk all formed part of his efforts to revamp the old system and we will not be far wrong in seeing in the constitution produced by Orlyk after Mazeppa's death the results of Mazeppa's own thoughts and his contact with his new friends.

Mazeppa was very weary. The loss of Baturyn came back to him again and again. His difficulties seemed at times insurmountable. He knew the growing weakness of the Swedish army but he was encouraged by the steady drift of Ukrainians to his own cause. He felt that he was slowly but surely winning his greatest battle and putting Ukraine on something like a permanent footing. But would he live to see the success of this conception?

CHAPTER TWENTY

POLTAVA

The campaign of Charles during the winter in the Land of Free Communes had perhaps shown him that it was rash with his reduced Swedish army to push on against Moscow and entangle himself in the middle of Russia. At the same time the accession of the Zaporozhians opened new possibilities of victory, for it turned his eyes to the south. It was the Poles who had first proposed an alliance with the Turks and Tatars but they had done it largely to induce the King to leave Polish territory, especially as they had shown no enthusiasm for joining in the campaign.

Now it was Mazeppa's turn to stress this new strategy. The aged Hetman could remember as none of the Swedes the long series of negotiations between the grandfather of Charles and Khmelnytsky. He knew the results of the plans of Doroshenko and even though they had proved disastrous, the situation would have been different with Sweden actively concerned. He did not perhaps go as far as Khmelnytsky who had at one time dreamed of a great Orthodox state which would include the Christians of the Ottoman Empire but as the leader of an independent Ukraine, he saw the possibilities in an alliance with the Mohammedans.

Peter was greatly worried by the prospects. He had, it is true, destroyed the Sich and he tried to follow up his victory by neutralizing the Moslem world. He instructed his representative in Constantinople, Peter Tolstoy, to bribe as many as possible of the Turkish advisers. He himself spent the winter on the lower Don and pretended from there to threaten the Tatars by preparing an expedition against them but this was only a feint and in the spring he moved his troops back to the north.

The key to the situation was Poltava, the only fortified post in central and southern Ukraine still in Muscovite hands. The Zaporozhians pointed out its importance and surrounded it at once with the bulk of their forces as soon as they joined Mazeppa. Located on the River Vorskla, it blocked the direct route between the Swedish-Ukrainian forces and Turkey and the Crimea. If it fell to Charles, the Muscovite position at the Sich would become untenable and the line of the Dnieper could be easily opened. It would likewise expose the entire southern border of Moscow. It would give Charles a new method of securing supplies by sea from Sweden, once he had won over the Sultan and Mazeppa had no doubt that this could be done.

All these possibilities made the southward movement of Charles a far more reasonable measure than it seemed to many of the Swedes who thought it a rash adventure but it was the one way to repair the damage done by the defeat of Loewenhaupt. It was also a tribute to the strategic ability of Mazeppa who warmly supported it.

The one possible question was the type of troops that should be used. Charles appreciated too well his infantry and cavalry. Mazeppa overstressed the importance of the Kozak tactics. Neither side yielded to the other and they agreed to disagree.

Early in the spring, the Swedes moved toward Poltava to support the Zaporozhians. Charles at first decided upon regular siege operations but his shortage of munitions made this impracticable and he began to stress more informal operations in which the Kozaks were more at home. Charles' methods seemed wise and apparently Poltava was destined to fall during the summer.

Peter and Menshikov saw the danger and they decided to force the issue. Early in June Menshikov moved his troops toward Poltava and a few days later Peter arrived with the regiments from the lower Don.

Menshikov was sure that he could conquer the Swedes in a pitched battle, for the Muscovites had overwhelming forces. Peter was not so confident. He had seen Charles too often pull victory out of even more difficult situations and he dreaded to risk everything on a single battle. Charles had no intention of standing on the defensive.

Then came the catastrophe which determined the outcome of the battle. On June 28, Charles fell into a Muscovite ambush while he was reconnoitering. A bullet struck him in the foot and penetrated it from toe to heel. Charles fell from his horse but by a superhuman effort he was able to remount and escape. It incapacitated him for active duty. Gangrene set in and for several days it was uncertain whether he would live or die. When his healthy constitution pulled him through, he found it impossible to sit on a horse and he had himself carried around on a litter to encourage his men.

Peter learned of this and on July 6 the Muscovite army crossed the Vorskla and fortified a position about two miles from the Swedish camp. Even Peter hesitated. He had put his army in a precarious situation and Charles realized the possibility of throwing it back into the river.

The Swedish King was not disturbed by the numerical superiority of Peter's forces. The Tsar had with him some 75,000 men but the majority were rather poorly trained and of indifferent morale. Charles, excluding detachments, camp guards and Kozaks, had scarcely 20,000 Swedish veterans on whom he chiefly relied. It was barely half the gallant army which he had led across the Vistula two years before. He had perhaps 15,000 Kozaks but they figured little in his plans for the battle. The issue was to be decided by the Swedes and the Muscovites.

The great fact was that Charles could not lead the attack in person. He made the plans but he handed over the actual field command to Marshal Rehnskiold, one of his better officers. Rehnskiold was not Charles. Like all of Charles' generals, he was brave and accurate and obedient but he did not have the magnetic gift of leadership and of improvisation which had served the King on so many hard fought fields.

Peter knew that the attack was coming. He redoubled his denunciations of Mazeppa for daring to try to tear Ukraine from Russia and make it independent. He outdid himself in his use of abusive language but he did not repeat the statement that Mazeppa

was merely working for Poland. That was too threadbare and obviously untrue to serve his purposes any longer.

On the morning of July 8, the Swedes moved to the attack.
The forces of General Axel Sparre were to attack the Muscovite
left and those of Roos the right. In the beginning of the battle
Sparre's troops cut through the Russian lines and somewhat later Roos
repeated on the right. The Muscovite infantry broke. Their cavalry
started to flee and a panic or near-panic ran through the camp.
Peter himself was ready to concede defeat and horses were brought
for him and his staff to recross the Vorskla. Then something happened.

Part of the Swedish forces in pursuit became entangled in a
small piece of woodland, where their rigid discipline and close
order put them at a disadvantage. Had Charles been in command,
he would have known what to do. Rehnskiold did not have the
imagination. Count Piper ordered the cavalry of General Kreutz
to pursue the fleeing enemy. He had the consent of the King but
Rehnskiold considered it an insult to his ability to command and
countermanded the order. The dispute was referred to the King
who supported Rehnskiold but these few minutes were fatal. The
Muscovites began to rally and Peter ordered Menshikov with 10,000
troops to launch a counterattack. This succeeded and the Swedes
were thrown in their turn into disorder.

Charles could not remain inactive and at this moment he ordered
his halberdiers to carry him on his litter into the thick of the action.
They did so but before he could rally his men, the troops carrying
him were cut down and the litter fell. It gave rise to the belief that
he had been killed and as the rumor of his death ran through the
already hesitating Swedes, they completely broke and fled. Finally
in a last desperate effort the wounded King had himself mounted
his horse but it was too late.

He could only rally some of the fugitives and try to withdraw in
some order from the fatal field. It was almost impossible. The
defeat became a rout. Many of the closest associates of the King,
even his secretary Piper, were taken prisoner. The Swedes suffered

about 5,000 casualties and many of the survivors were more or less badly wounded.

Within a few hours the Swedish Empire was lost. Charles knew it at once and he realized that this defeat in far off Ukraine had destroyed once and for all what he and his ancestors had been trying to accomplish. The Baltic would not become a Swedish lake. Sweden had been cut back to size and could no longer proudly hope to be one of the leading nations of Europe.

The war made the Russian Empire. It ended the long struggle of the Tsars to secure a foothold on the Baltic. A half century earlier Moscow had secured the upper hand over Poland. Poltava and the failure of Poland to support Charles energetically had thrown that country entirely under Russian domination. Peter was now free to develop his policy as he would, to build his new capital of St. Petersburg, and he had only to deal with a weakened Turkey and that Turkey was far from the empire that a quarter century earlier had even threatened Vienna and central Europe.

The battle destroyed Ukraine. Gone were all of Mazeppa's hopes. Gone was the power of the Zaporozhian Host. The dreams of the Ukrainians from the time of Khmelnytsky were blasted for good and all and Peter was free to dispose of the country and the population as he would.

Mazeppa had followed the course of the battle but had stayed in his tent. He was an old man and weary, despite the energy with which he had thrown himself into the cause of the independence of his country. He was not the dashing leader of a half century before. In addition he was pained by what was really a fratricidal strife. Skoropadsky and his Kozaks were actively engaged on the side of Peter. Many of his best friends had been forced to serve against the Host or had thrown in their lot with the Muscovites and the old Hetman did not want to see their shame.

At the first news of the change of fortune, he came out of his tent and mounted his horse. He hurried to the side of the Swedish King, for he knew that with the debacle, it would be he and his

Kozaks who alone could extricate Charles from the dangers that surrounded him.

In the first moments of his defeat Charles decided to go to Turkey and renew the war from there. The Kozaks were to escort him and the remnants of his army. They knew every mile of the road from Poltava to the Black Sea. It was not for nothing that for more than a century they had ranged over the boundless steppes, until they were as familiar with them as with their own fields. How many times had the Hetman himself made that trip from Poltava to the Crimea or the Turkish borders! He could hardly say but in the crisis he found the strength to do it again.

Then Charles decided not to go. In his discouragement he planned to rally his few remaining men, use up his almost exhausted supplies of ammunition and hurl himself against the Russian lines to seek for death. He would not be humiliated by surrendering to Peter.

There was no choice for Mazeppa and the Kozaks. The memories of the massacres at Baturyn and the Sich were too vivid. Mazeppa had no doubt of the fate of all the men who fell into Peter's hands. The Tsar had made that clear and the Hetman knew that he had given orders to take him alive and subject him to the severest tortures. He had no intention of being slaughtered to make a Muscovite holiday.

The staff of Charles joined in their petitions to the King to follow the advice of Mazeppa and to retreat to the south. Precious hours were wasted but finally the King yielded and the party started down the Vorskla toward the Dnieper, but it was a sad and discouraged march.

They were saved only by the actions of Peter. He broke off pursuit in the idea that Charles was dead, so as to celebrate his victory. As a Western monarch, he entertained at the dinner not only his own officers but all of the captured Swedes who had fallen into his hands. He glorified them and honored them as his teachers and entertained them royally, the while he slipped out to witness the tortures of all the Kozaks who had fallen into his hands. To them he was the traditional Russian Tsar who knew no mercy, no pardon and could only be satisfied by the sight of blood.

This feast, conducted in Peter's own manner, gave the fugitives nearly a day's advantage but much of this was lost, when the party lost its way in a forest and floundered around for several hours. Even this had its advantages for gradually the King was joined by scattered detachments of his forces which had succeeded in escaping. Under the protection of Kozak scouts, they were guided together and once again there was something that might be called a Swedish army but it was a mass of discouraged and despairing fugitives and not that proud force which had charged at Poltava such a short time before.

On the 9th, the King had ordered burned all the archives and papers of the expedition and all documents that might in any degree be useful to the Russians if they were captured; the tents were burned, and the horses were used for the infantry so as to facilitate their escape. It was at this time that all the materials rescued from Baturyn disappeared and this has left us with no answer to many of the most important questions about the life of the Hetman.

By the morning of July 10, the King was only a few hours ahead of the cavalry of Menshikov who had taken up the pursuit. At the village of Kobelyaky the Swedish rearguard made a stand and once more at the cost of their own lives, they held up the Russian cavalry and allowed the King to gain a few hours.

On the evening of the 10th, the fugitives reached the Dnieper at the mouth of the Vorskla. Again their hopes sank, for the Russians had been ahead of them and had destroyed all the boats. They had removed the cables that were used in ferrying across the river and had done everything to make a crossing impossible. Charles decided that he would go no further. He planned again a last stand to find death on the field of battle. It was a mad decision for he knew that Menshikov could take his time and bring up fresh troops in overwhelming force before he risked an attack. By now the Swedes numbered but 10,000 men.

Again Mazeppa and the Kozaks solved the problem. Ferries meant little to them. They raised some of the sunken boats. They built wooden platforms on which they placed the carriages of Charles and some of his associates. Then they harnessed their horses to these platforms with long ropes and rode them into the river. They swam their steeds across and towed the boats after them. By midnight the royal party, now reduced to some of the higher officers, the halberdiers and about one hundred horsemen, were across the Dnieper.

The King left the rest of the Swedes on the east bank under the command of Loewenhaupt who had promised not to surrender. What were they to do? Charles had given their commander abundant discretion but he apparently hoped that they would make their way along the bank, while he went on to Turkey to seek new allies to come to their rescue. The army did not get far.

Menshikov soon arrived and demanded the surrender of the entire force. Loewenhaupt played for time, for he knew that with each hour the King was moving further and further from the scene. Menshikov knew it too and was inexorable in demanding surrender. Finally Loewenhaupt put the question to a vote of his soldiers. Some of the regiments insisted upon fighting but they were in a hopeless minority, for the men were sick of the campaign and they voted to accept the offer. As always, Menshikov treated the Swedes well and pardoned them.

It was very different with the Kozaks. Menshikov denied them the rights of combatants and Loewenhaupt did not insist. All who were taken were tortured to death as traitors. Only a few who at the first moment had dashed their horses into the Dnieper were able to make their escape but the majority who tried it were drowned.

Charles was in despair. His fortunes seemed ruined. He was in a strange land without an army. He was listless and indecisive. His wound was still troubling him and he drove along in his carriage helpless and undecided but with each day his feelings revived and by the time that he reached Turkey, he had recovered most of his poise and self-control.

It was quite the reverse with Mazeppa. Though he was nearly eighty, he seemed tireless. Early and late he was on horseback. He set out the pickets when the party halted. He thought of everything. He was everywhere. He was the heart and soul of the retreat and his strength seemed limitless.

What did he think as he pressed on? He had crossed these steppes with Golitsyn. He had crossed them for Peter. He had travelled to the Khan for Doroshenko. He had been captured here by Sirko. Where were all those men? They had all passed the toilsome way to Siberia as prisoners and exiles, if they had not first been executed. Golitsyn was gone, Doroshenko, Samoylovych. One and all had learned what confidence to place in the word of a Russian Tsar. Loyalty was disregarded, when it suited the Muscovite whim. Faith and fidelity were no guarantee of friendly treatment, if slander or denunciation were more profitable to the powers that be.

Now he was going into exile. He could not fail to realize that the cause of Ukraine was lost but he was going into exile as Hetman and in this last hour he still had a mission. He had to save his friend and ally, Charles XII of Sweden. His Kozak honor, his honor as Hetman demanded it,—yes and the possible chance that the King might ultimately succeed in his plans for a grand alliance against Peter and then there would be a hope for Ukraine. So he forced his body to obey his will and he drove his Kozaks on and on. He revived the spirit of the old Hetmans, the men who had dared the impossible and flying from the Muscovite pursuit, he raised the Kozak endurance to a new level. His conduct of the retreat was in the best traditions of the old Kozak raiders and no one would have said that the man who was everywhere, who thought of everything, was almost eighty years old, was that formal and even pompous Hetman who had seemed so careless of everything except his works of art and his personal luxury. It was another Mazeppa that led the retreat or was it the old Mazeppa set free from the degrading need of flattery and serving petty masters?

He had advised Charles to get across the open steppe to Bendery at the mouth of the Dniester, for that was the nearest place of safety but it was a long and arduous journey and if the danger of Muscovite pursuit grew less, the physical strain increased as the weary Swedes pushed on in the blazing summer heat.

There was grass for the horses but the men did not dare for some days to take time for hunting and when they did finally venture to pause long enough, the Swedes could not roast their game because of the lack of fire and equipment. The Kozaks, accustomed to the steppes, showed them how to construct serviceable cooking arrangements out of trash and grass.

Fortunately on the 15th, the party came across a train of carts carrying salt from Bratslav to Ukraine. The Kozaks commandeered the whole, including the horses and they secured a considerable amount of supplies which came in handy on their long journey.

A week had passed since the battle and the fugitives began to breathe more freely. The Muscovite pursuit was being slowed, for the Russians were all too aware of the risks that even a large party ran in the steppes against the more experienced Kozaks. They had seen too many cases of fires set in the dry grass to wreck an invading force to plunge madly ahead, even after men as prominent as Charles and Mazeppa. They did not want to fight the Kozaks on their own ground and even Menshikov drew back at the thought.

As it became certain that the party was going to win through, the spirit of the King began to revive. The depression that had hung over him since the battle, melted away. His wound was healing and he felt that in a short time he would be again in a position to renew the war, especially if he could secure new allies. He began to dream again of what he would do, what moves he would make, with whom he would get into contact.

It was the opposite with Mazeppa. Ever since he had decided to make an open break with Peter, he had roused himself to unaccustomed energy. The years had fallen away from him that night at Borzna, when he had dashed off with his staff on his wild ride to Baturyn. For the week since the battle he had had almost no

rest. He had attended himself to every detail. He had been the spirit
and the heart of the march. Now as he thought of the future and
could begin to relax, the years came back. Day by day he grew
perceptibly weaker. He was still the commander but with the danger receding into the background and becoming more remote,
he allowed more power to his subordinates. He dismounted and
continued the journey in one of the carriages with some Ukrainian
ladies who were making the hazardous trip. One of these was
probably the widow of his nephew, Hanna Obidovska.

He knew that for him there was no future. Even if the most
glowing hopes of Charles were to be carried out, he would not
be there to see them. He did not have the physical strength to
share the King's triumph, no matter how soon it came. He had left
Ukraine for the last time. He had done his best and he had
failed.

And his country? He knew that Peter would never allow another Hetman to have any real power. Skoropadsky was only a
figurehead, a man who was not in a position to object to any restrictions that Peter saw fit to impose and who would not struggle for
those rights and privileges which had always been dear to the Kozak
heart. In every real sense of the word, he was the last Hetman
worthy of the name and it was a depressing thought.

As the party came near the Turkish border, the King sent
ahead General Poniatowski, the ambassador from King Stanislaw,
his secretary Klinkovstrem and a Kozak officer to meet the seraskier
and Pasha of Ochakiv and arrange for entrance into the Turkish
Empire. They were indeed the harbingers of bad news for no word
of the defeat had been carried across the steppes and it seemed
inconceivable that the great and ever victorious conquerer, the Lion
of the North, Charles XII, was approaching as a defeated fugitive.
The Pasha did not want him in his territory. He was still less
willing to offer shelter for the Hetman who had so often worsted
him in both arms and diplomacy.

Still the Pasha could not say this openly and so he offered to
send one boat for the King to bring him across the River Buh

but he delayed his answer on all other questions and in the meanwhile he sent a message to the Sultan in Constantinople. He hoped that during this delay the Muscovite forces would put in an appearance and free him from the necessity of answering. He charged fantastic prices for food and supplies which the Greek and Armenian merchants took across the river and which were eagerly snapped up by the starving and exhausted Swedes. It was soon clear that the Pasha was more interested in obtaining money than in giving help.

Charles would not brook the delay, for he realized that sooner or later the Muscovites under Menshikov would put in an appearance. He ordered the Swedes to seize the boats and crossed almost by force, and then paid the owners well for their use. The Kozaks swam their horses across but a considerable number of Swedes who were among the last to cross fell into Muscovite hands.

Once safe in the Ottoman Empire, the group continued its weary way. They finally reached Ochakiv. By now the Pasha had heard from Constantinople and had received definite orders to admit both the Swedes and Kozaks. He tried to be friendly but Charles would not trust him again and instead of entering the city, he pitched his camp in a little village about two miles away. Mazeppa and the Kozaks camped near by, near Lake Adgigol on a site which the Kozaks had frequently used to hide their boats when they made forays into the Empire. All this did not profit the Pasha, for as soon as Charles reached his destination of Bendery he exerted his influence through his allies and friends in the Turkish capital and the Pasha was summarily removed.

A few days of rest and the little party went on to their destination, the city of Bendery on the lower Dniester. On August 1, they finally reached this and they settled down to await developments.

The handling of this retreat was the last and perhaps the greatest military feat of Mazeppa's life. With a small band of faithful Kozaks, he had snatched the King of Sweden, wounded and despairing, almost out of the middle of the Tsar's armies and had carried him hundreds of miles to safety. He had done it under the force of habit, by the accumulated experiences of the past, and he had put into it all that remained to him of life. He had only one task left, to provide for the future of his faithful followers and to arrange things so that they would have a chance in case there came a turn in the wheel of fortune. The future of Ukraine, if there was to be one, was in the hands of the exiles. There lay its traditions, its hopes and its future, for so long as the Russian Empire was to continue, the Kozaks at home could take no initiative. It would be all that they could do to maintain their own positions silently and quietly. It was therefore, in Mazeppa's eyes, his final work to try to link the future of Ukraine with all of those forces that were working to thwart the steady advance of the Muscovites to the east, west, north and south.

CHAPTER TWENTY-ONE

THE END OF THE TRAIL

On August 1, 1709, Charles and Mazeppa reached Bendery. Here the Turkish authorities received them kindly and hospitably and with due regard for their rank. The physical hardships of the journey were over. They were for the moment safe, and it was now their task to rebuild their shattered forces and to plan their next moves.

Charles took up his residence in Bendery and created there a miniature court and camp. He lived simply but with dignity and plunged into the task of recouping his fortunes. Mazeppa and his Kozaks settled down in the neighboring village of Varnytsya. For a while he maintained another centre in Jassy, where he sent Orlyk for some days but he could not get along without him and Orlyk soon returned to Varnytsya.

Bendery became the centre of furious diplomatic activity. The arrival of Charles in Turkey had put him into an advantageous position and he showed remarkable diplomatic skill. Even before he had reached Bendery, he had sent a joint Swedish-Kozak mission to the Khan of the Crimea to urge him to attack Moscow and to try to recover Azov and the other regions which Peter had taken from him. His missions to Constantinople, urging the Sultan to declare war, slowly had effect and the Sultan began to look even more favorably on the plans of Charles.

The Swedish King found other supporters. The War of the Spanish Succession was still going on in the west of Europe, but it was not confined to that one continent. The French and the British were locked in struggle in Asia and in America, where the people of the Thirteen Colonies called it Queen Anne's War. There was fighting in Canada, there was fighting in India, and everywhere the ramifications of that war took in all kinds of local and apparently isolated interests. The French were supporting King

Stanislaw against Peter and while they had been inclined to criticize Charles for not leading his armies into Western Europe, now that he was in Constantinople, they did everything to win him a hearing with the Sultan and tried to coordinate their plans with his. Finally they added their influence to his and induced the Sultan to declare war.

Peter for his part knew that by the victory of Poltava he had wiped out the Swedish hold on the east shore of the Baltic and that his position there was secure. He knew that he had now the whole of Poland in his power. Yet he had too healthy a respect for the military skill of Charles to see unmoved Charles rebuilding a military alliance against him with Constantinople as the centre but he was still determined that he was going to secure the person of Mazeppa in one way or another.

He sent Peter Tolstoy, his envoy to the Sultan, to Bendery to try to make peace with Charles and he offered advantageous terms but always on the one condition that the King would break his alliance with Mazeppa and hand the Hetman and the Kozaks over to him for his personal vengeance.

In making this demand he was judging Charles by his own standards of honor and of decency. Charles indignantly refused. He was a personal friend of the Hetman, he knew that it was the Hetman and the Kozaks who had won his own safety and had carried him across the steppes and saved him from falling into the hands of Peter and he was not the man to profit by treason and by breaking his sworn word. Tolstoy had to return to Constantinople and admit his mission a failure.

The envoy next approached the Turkish authorities and tried bribery. He sought to have Charles expelled from the country and he demanded also the handing over of Mazeppa and his men. Peter was known to be avaricious and miserly but he commissioned Tolstoy to pay unprecedentedly large sums to the advisers of the Sultan, if only he could secure what he wished. He approached the Grand Vizier. He offered even larger sums to the Grand Mufti, the spiritual adviser of the Sultan as Caliph, to bid him accede to Peter in the terms of Mohammedan law.

The Hetman could not fail to know of these intrigues and to be disturbed by them. He knew the venality of many of the Turkish officials and their inability to resist these enormous bribes. He knew that his hope lay in Charles and he was amazed at the ingenuity of his friends. In the course of the next few months, Charles not only refused to abandon the old Hetman, but his envoys in Constantinople, Neugebauer and Poniatowski, worked so effectively with French help that when Tolstoy appeared with still more bribes and demands and thought that he was winning, he landed in a Turkish prison and the Sultan declared war on Peter.

Yet the Sultan did not make use of the military talents of Charles who remained half guest, half hostage and rather under surveillance. Success at times seemed near but it always eluded him. When in 1711 Peter made a rash campaign to the south, he found himself trapped near the mouth of the River Prut. Gold and treachery saved him from the humiliation of capture by the Turks but as it was, he had to return to the Khan of the Crimea the city of Azov and all the conquests which he had made with the aid of Mazeppa. He had to promise in ambiguous terms to evacuate Ukraine and to restore the Zaporozhian Host, promises which he never intended to and did not carry out, once he was out of the trap. Then Charles, whose advice had been systematically ignored, decided to return home and in 1715 he stealthily left Bendery and made his way back to Sweden and was followed by Orlyk and his trusted Ukrainian and Swedish advisers.

Mazeppa was not with him. As we have mentioned, when Charles went to Bendery, Mazeppa set up his headquarters near by at Varnytsya and to this point and also to Jassy there straggled in a steady stream of Kozaks, who in one way or another had escaped Peter's torture chambers. Some had made their way over the pathless steppe by long detours from the catastrophe of Poltava. Others had been away at the time of the capture of the Sich and had learned of the massacre and instead of falling into the trap set

by Peter, they had drifted south to safety in the Ottoman Empire
or the domains of the Khan of the Crimea. They rallied to the
cause of the Hetman. Still others escaped the various purges and
likewise came to the new Kozak centre.

But Mazeppa's course was run. That last journey across the
steppe was the last physical event of his career and from the time
when he reached Varnytsya he took to his bed and never again left
it. His body failed steadily. His mind remained clear as he worked
constantly for the welfare and safety of his men and the salvation
of the Host and Ukraine.

His old friendship with Charles was unbroken. Every few days
the King rode over to see him and every day sent a messenger to
inquire about his health. Mazeppa put at his disposal his vast
knowledge of the ways of the Turks and Tatars and his familiarity
through long years with the tangled skein of diplomatic relations
from the time of Khmelnytsky and even before. He had succeeded
in saving a considerable part of the treasure which he had carried
from Baturyn and he freely put this at the disposal of the King.
He lent him at least 60,000 ducats for his necessary expenses during the early weeks when Charles was trying to establish himself
in Turkey.

By the end of September, it was obvious that the old man, worn
out by his exertions and by the constant threat of Russian intrigues,
could not last much longer. The Kozaks summoned an Orthodox
priest from Jassy to wait for the end and give him the last rites of
the Church. The Hetman begged Charles to assign to him a permanent liaison officer and was overjoyed to see Soldan appointed, for
he had been the chief adviser of the King on Ukrainian affairs;
he spoke Ukrainian and knew how to handle both the Swedes and
the Kozaks. Yet with death staring him in the face, Mazeppa could
still joke in his mildly pedantic manner and compare his fate to
that of the Roman poet Ovid who in his last years had been exiled
from Rome to die on the coast of the Black Sea in Ukraine.

A few days later and even this became impossible. Mazeppa
sank into semi-consciousness and muttered constantly incoherent

phrases about his mother, his treasure and a small chest of documents which should not be allowed to fall into the hands of the
Turks. That chest which really existed has disappeared and we can
only speculate what these precious papers were. On the afternoon
of October 2 Charles rode over to bid his friend farewell but
Mazeppa was already in a coma and did not recognize him.

Later that night of October 2, the Hetman passed away. He
was dying in exile but he was dying as Hetman. He was dying a
natural death as a free man and he was the first Hetman since
Bohdan Khmelnytsky of whom this could be said. Some as Vyhovsky
had been murdered in rebellions. Others had been executed by
the Poles. The vast majority and this included all those whom he
had known most intimately, Doroshenko, Mnohohrishny, Samoylovych, had perished in Muscovite prisons or in Siberia. They had
been punished for acts of treason which they had not committed.
After years of vacillation, Mazeppa had declared himself openly
for the freedom of Ukraine and while he had lost and was a
fugitive in exile, he still had with him the insignia of the Hetman,
he had found a hearing for the cause of his country abroad and had
been recognized as an independent sovereign by all the foes of
Moscow. He could feel that he had not lived his life in vain.

During his last hours, he was attended by his nephew Voynarovsky, by Orlyk, by Soldan and by the priest. His end was peaceful
and about ten o'clock in the evening he breathed his last.

For more than twenty-four hours a violent storm raged over
Varnytsya. The rain came down in sheets but it did not scatter
the crowd of weeping Kozaks who had gathered outside the Hetman's tent to await the sad news. Then Orlyk came out, lowered
the personal standard of the Hetman and made the fateful an-
nouncement that His Most Serene Highness, Ivan Mazeppa, Hetman
of the Zaporozhian Host, had passed away. The guns of the fortress
of Bendery boomed out the salute prescribed by international law
and courtesy for the death of a sovereign monarch.

There was not a person in the crowd that did not realize that
with the death of the Hetman an era had come to an end. Mazeppa

had seen the rise of the Hetman State, he had played an important
role in its history for nearly fifty years, and he had risen to his
real stature at the end. He had won in that last year more love
and affection than he had known in his entire life, for he had
stood out as the true representative of the Kozak ideals. Who
could take his place? What would happen next to Ukraine and
the Host? No one knew and the thought of the national misfortune blended with the feeling of personal loss.

On October 4, the funeral of the Hetman was held not in
Bendery but across the border in Moldavia. A stately and formal
procession escorted the remains to the little Orthodox Church that
had been selected for the service. At its head were Swedish
trombones and Kozak buglers. Then came the symbols of the
Hetman, the mace, the standard and the horsetail bunchuk. A
caisson with six white horses bore the body. Then came Mazeppa's
horse and his sword. Charles XII headed the procession with his
staff and the ambassadors accredited to him, the representatives of
the Ottoman government in Bendery and the Princes of Moldavia
and Wallachia. They were followed by the Kozak officers, including Kost Hordiyenko, the Koshovy Otaman of the Zaporozhian
Sich, and the entire Kozak army. The wives of the Ukrainian
officers and men who had come into exile with their husbands
followed and then came a vast crowd of people of all nationalities
who had gathered from far and near for the occasion.

After the service, Orlyk delivered a funeral oration in Latin and
outlined his policy for the future.

"This illustrious and venerated chief whose great age has left
him without descendants, who possessed vast wealth, sacrificed everything to give his country its liberty. He did not hesitate to renounce everything which could be dear to him on this earth; he
gave his very life that his country could be saved from the Muscovite
yoke.

"Alas! the decree of Fate has come to strike down here in a
foreign land the illustrious Hetman, His Serene Highness, Ivan
Mazeppa, whose name will live eternally with an immortal glory

in the memory of our people, for he wished to allow it to develop, in full liberty, its infinite possibilities. Let neither the army nor the people despair; our cause is just and a just cause always triumphs in the end.

"No one will ever be so great in our country as Mazeppa; but although we are unworthy to pursue the enterprise undertaken by our chief of glorious memory, we will continue to guide amid the shoals and storms the Kozak vessel to the harbor of liberty. But it is to you, O King, that we appeal before the coffin of our illustrious chief. We hope that you will aid the Kozak bark. Magnificent Lion, you will oppose your breast to the Muscovite who is subjugating and tyrannizing over our Ukraine."

It was an extrordinary scene, a strange blending of the Eastern and Western traditions but it was symbolic of the wide ramifications and complications of the Ukrainian problem. Here were gathered around the body of the great Hetman, Charles XII of Sweden, the greatest soldier of the day, and representatives of France, the Sultan, the Khan of the Crimea, Poles, Greeks, Romanians and men of all nationalities. Here were the armed forces of Ukraine, Sweden and Turkey. All had come together to pay a last tribute to the man who had dared to defy the imperialism of Moscow and all felt themselves equally menaced by the aggressive designs of Peter. It was a proof, if proof were needed, that the Kozaks and Ukraine held a key position in the effort to keep Moscow within proper bounds.

The last speeches were made, the last courtesies shown to the departed and the King and his officials withdrew. A detachment of Kozaks moved off to escort the body of their leader to the Monastery of St. George in Galatz on the Danube. There in a brick vault which the Kozaks built themselves under the choir of the church, the Hetman was laid to rest and over his grave was placed a simple slab with merely his name and a representation of his arms, perhaps a representation of the Archangel Michael, the symbol of the Zaporozhian army.

Yet his body was not to rest in peace. Two years later, during the war between Turkey and Peter, a detachment of Turkish soldiers in quest of booty broke into the vault. They had the idea that the treasures of the Hetman had been buried with him. A Ukrainian detachment again under the command of Orlyk found the body and restored it to its grave but they left the broken slab as a mute memorial to the outrage.

More than a hundred years later, when the memory of the Hetman had grown dim, the relatives of a Moldavian boyar who had been a great benefactor of the monastery, paid lavishly to have his body placed in the same vault. Then they changed their mind and in moving the new corpse, they disturbed the old. One of the Princes Ghika removed the slab and since then it has been lost to history.

So much for the body of the Hetman. But the Ukrainian people were not satisfied. Legends arose about the old Hetman. Some claimed that he had been poisoned by a Greek acting in the interests of Russia. Others repeated a wilder and more improbable story that he had escaped from Bendery, that he had only pretended to die and that he had returned in disguise to live out his days as a nameless monk in that great Ukrainian shrine, the Pecherska Lavra in Kiev.

His worldly possessions and the Host still remained. The Turks tried to secure the money but the personal intervention of Charles prevented this and the remains of his fortune were left in Kozak possession.

Then came a new dispute. There were still two barrels of ducats and of jewels. Voynarovsky, the elegant nephew of the Hetman, laid claim to them as his personal estate. He was opposed by the Kozak leaders and on October 7, Ivan Lomykovsky, the Quartermaster General, Pylyp Orlyk, the General Secretary, Dmytro Horlenko, the Colonel of the Pryluky Regiment, Fedir Myrovych, the bearer of the bunchuk and Kostyatyn Hordiyenko, the Koshovy Otaman of the Lower Zaporozhian Army (the Sich) signed an appeal to Charles to turn over to them the treasure on the ground that it was the property of the Kozak Host and was needed to reform the organization and continue its work of liberating Ukraine.

Both sides stated their case in long briefs and from these documents we can learn much of the sources of the enormous wealth that the Hetman had amassed. On his accession to the position of Hetman, he had received the wealth of Bryukhovetsky, Mnohohrishny and Samoylovych and this should have gone to his successor. All were willing to let Voynarovsky have it and assume the post of Hetman but he refused that burdensome condition. It had long been evident that whatever Mazeppa had wished for him, it was not to make him Hetman in his place. The King finally awarded the bulk of the fortune to Voynarovsky and he withdrew from the Host. He continued to work for Ukraine in his elegant, often over-artistic and hedonistic way until he was betrayed into the hands of Moscow and ended his days in Siberia.

Orlyk was of tougher stuff. In the spring of 1710 he was formally elected Hetman at Bendery. He took himself and his position seriously and for the next quarter of a century he was a familiar figure all over Europe, wherever there was the slightest possibility of forming a coalition against Russia. Now he was fighting at the head of a Kozak detachment in the wars between Turkey and Russia. Now he was invading Ukraine with small bodies of men, whenever there were disturbances along the western border. Now he was in Sweden with King Charles. Now his headquarters were in Salonika. Now he was in Paris and taking part in the councils of the King of France. Now he was here and there. Anywhere and everywhere he was the spokesman for his people and tried in every way possible to rouse Europe to the Russian menace.

Soon after his election as Hetman, he presented to the Kozaks the first written constitution for the population of Ukraine. For the first time he put into definite written shape a form of state organization, aristocratic to be sure, but still providing for the position of the Officers' Council and the General Assembly of the Kozaks. It was almost certainly the result of his association with

Mazeppa who in the last months of his life had finally come to realize that with the attainment of recognition by foreign governments, Ukraine could not maintain that free and easy system of administration which had been developed by the military needs of the Zaporozhian Sich and which would have taken a different shape if it had not been for foreign interference. Of course Orlyk's constitution, made abroad, always remained a dead letter, a stillborn child but in its contents it was one of the most progressive political documents of the early eighteenth century.

The Russian Tsars were always conscious of the danger from these Mazepyntsi, these followers of Mazeppa. They made every effort to wipe them out, arrest or murder them. They included them in the yearly repetition of the excommunication of their leader and even today under the Soviets the name of Mazeppa is always mentioned in connection with the great anti-Communist leaders of Ukraine, Hrushevsky, Petlyura, etc.

All this was a tribute to the real Mazeppa who had perished far from his native land. Russian poets and historians alike could blacken his character and berate his ability. They knew that he had struck a chord that would never cease resounding until Ukraine was free.

EPILOGUE

Few men have received such contradictory verdicts of history as has Ivan Mazeppa. The great Romantic poets of Western Europe as Lord Byron and Victor Hugo have written of him in terms of legends that could scarcely have been true. Russians of every political school have treated his very name as anathema and have pictured him either as a traitor or a hard-boiled and incompetent fool of no character but able to deceive and continue to deceive the two greatest men of the period, Peter I of Russia and Charles XII of Sweden. They have been blissfully unaware that their own picture either means the exposure of their idols or is a glowing tribute to their enemy.

In his lifetime both his friends and foes considered him an extraordinary person, a man of winning charm, of great learning, and with a real gift for leadership. In his old age, when he was thrown directly between Charles and Peter, he bore himself with a dignity, even in defeat, that continued to hide the fire that must have burned within him.

He lived a long and active life but much of it was and still is hidden in the shadows, for he had no opportunity to speak out fearlessly and boldly for what he believed. He was trained in the school of silence, to be a courtier whose one mission in life was to flatter and please his superiors and yet to carry out his own policies, even when they were directed against the men who held his fate in their hands. The very importance and difficulties of his post bound him to silence and secretiveness became second nature to him. It was his tragedy that it was only at the end that he could say what he thought. The records of his career and of his thoughts perished so far as they were written in the holocaust of Baturyn and the burning of his documents after the battle of Poltava. Nothing was left but the memories of his friends and they were forgotten or buried in the dust of archives, while his enemies fashioned a lay figure, an effigy on which they could pile unlimited abuse.

224

Mazeppa's task was to finish the work of Khmelnytsky and to turn the Zaporozhian Kozaks into the nucleus of a modern state. The Kozaks had started their course as valiant fighters for liberty as they saw it. They were free men who acknowledged no law but their own will. They feared no power, no enemy, not even death. They cared little or nothing for the established principles of settled life and administrative order. Like pioneers and frontiersmen everywhere, they were turbulent and unruly but they had an ideal, often inchoate and felt rather than expressed.

It was the task of the Hetmans to form out of them a state. Khmelnytsky commenced the task but he died in midcourse and no one was strong enough to complete it. No one was able to hold the disruptive elements in check and compete successfully in the hard and treacherous game of international politics.

Mazeppa came to power at a time when it seemed as if the standardizing autocratic methods of the tsars who were changing medieval Muscovy into the Russian Empire could not be withstood, when the Kozak liberties were being overwhelmed and resistance seemed hopeless. Silence and intrigue were his only weapons and he used them to the best of his knowledge. All this forced him into a peculiar position and laid him open to criticism on every side.

With it all, he was a gentleman of the Renaissance, with an appreciation of art and science. He was no democrat but where in Eastern Europe was there a line drawn between anarchic democracy and slavish autocracy? He could not open his heart to the ordinary Kozaks who wanted the former. He had to rely upon Peter who wanted the second. He could not trust his officers, especially after the denunciation of Kochubey. By himself he had to make in secret the necessary decisions and find himself the way of carrying them out. When the Zaporozhian Sich, for decades his most formidable opponent, voted to join him in his revolt against Peter, it was a sign that he had not forgotten the interests of his people and had not misjudged the spirit of the Kozaks.

The battle of Poltava destroyed his hopes and that battle was nearly a victory for the cause which he had espoused. He died far from his native land in exile, apparently a failure, as Peter adjudged him. Yet the very fury with which Peter pursued him, the very hatred that the Russians poured out upon him showed the narrow margin which separated him from success and the terror that he had inspired in his foes.

Can we be so sure today that Mazeppa lived in vain or that he followed a false ideal? We are all too familiar with the spectacle of democratic statesmen who have deserved well of their country, trying to flee from behind the iron curtain of Moscow's imperialistic Communism or ending their days in Siberian concentration camps or before firing squads. We are all too familiar with the abuse that is being hurled by the masters of the Kremlin on those desperate partisan bands who are struggling against overwhelming odds to preserve their national ideals and rights behind the iron curtain. We read almost every week the Russian Communist diatribes against Ukrainian nationalism and separatism which is systematically and repeatedly wiped out by fire and sword and the torture chamber and then miraculously rises again.

Mazeppa faced the eighteenth century version of this nightmare. He had seen the methods of Tsar Alexis, the Regent Sofia, and Peter I. He had concealed his feelings and his sympathies and held his ground, until Charles XII offered him at least a fighting chance to come out in the open and to win in open conflict.

His conduct, unsuccessful at the moment, meant more to his people than he could imagine. Mazeppa became a symbol to the Ukrainians of their own right to exist. He modified the old Kozak tradition and he started a new one which inspired the poems of Taras Shevchenko, the Ukrainian National Republic of 1917, the Ukrainian Insurgent Army of 1945, the new Ukrainian movement of the nineteenth and twentieth centuries and the present struggle for independence.

Dignified and magnificent, statuesque and silent, Mazeppa moved on his lonesome way. Perhaps he revealed himself only to his mother and to Orlyk, perhaps more personally to Motrya. We can never appreciate all that went on behind that rigid exterior; we can never understand all his anxieties and his emotions. His personal life, lived in the glare of publicity, under the eyes of friends and enemies, still remains a riddle. History has justified him and his beliefs. The cold war of the present is still following the same course that Ivan Mazeppa took and there can be no peace until his ideals for his country triumph and a Ukraine that is in the United Nations is able to speak there with its own voice and not through the words and agents of Moscow. When that time comes, the forms in which Mazeppa thought may be antiquated but his conception of liberty under law will not be. When that time comes, Mazeppa will appear in his full stature. Not only his people but the world will recognize him as he was seen by Orlyk and his co-workers and then with all his faults, his pedantry, and his defects Ivan Mazeppa will appear as an ardent patriot and the great Hetman of Ukraine.

BIBLIOGRAPHY

ANDRUSYAK, M.—*Mazeppa and the Left Bank*—Lviv, 1938.

BORSCHAK, Ilie et MARTEL, RENE—*Vie de Mazeppa*—Paris, 1931.

Entsyklopediya Ukrayinoznavstva—Munich, Paris, New York, 1949.

Great History of Ukraine, edited by I. TYKTOR—Winnipeg.

HRUSHEVSKY, M.—*History of Ukraine*—New Haven, 1941.

KOSTOMAROV, N.—*Mazeppa and the Mazepintsy* (Collected Works, Vol. XVI)—Moscow, 1883.

KRUPNYCKYJ, BORIS—*Hetman Mazeppa und seine Zeit*—Berlin, 1942.

KRUPNYTSKY, BORIS—*The Swedish-Ukrainian Treaties of Alliance 1708-1709*—The Ukrainian Quarterly, Vol. XII, pp. 47-57.

LUCIW, WASYL—*Hetman Ivan Mazeppa*—Toronto, 1954.

MANNING, C. A.—*The Story of Ukraine*—New York, 1947.

MAZEPPA—*Vols. I and II, Ukrainian Scientific Institute*—Warsaw, 1938-39.

YAKOVLIV, A.—*Ukrainian-Muscovite Treaties in the XVII and XVIII Centuries*—Warsaw, 1934.

INDEX

229